**on
Europe**

Twain
on
Europe

HESPERUS
'on'

Published by Hesperus Press Limited
28 Mortimer Street, London W1W 7RD
www.hesperuspress.com

Extracts taken from *Innocents Abroad* (1869), *A Tramp Abroad* (1880) and
First published by Hesperus Press Limited, 2013

Typeset by Madeline Meckiffe
Printed in Great Britain by CPI Group (UK) Ltd

isbn: 978-1-84391-621-5

Contents

France 7

Italy 35

Spain 107

Greece 115

Germany 125

Switzerland 157

Notes 165

Biographical note 166

France

Toward nightfall the next evening, we steamed into the great artificial harbor of this noble city of Marseilles, and saw the dying sunlight gild its clustering spires and ramparts, and flood its leagues of environing verdure with a mellow radiance that touched with an added charm the white villas that flecked the landscape far and near.

There were no stages out, and we could not get on the pier from the ship. It was annoying. We were full of enthusiasm – we wanted to see France! Just at nightfall our party of three contracted with a waterman for the privilege of using his boat as a bridge – its stern was at our companion ladder and its bow touched the pier. We got in and the fellow backed out into the harbor. I told him in French that all we wanted was to walk over his thwarts and step ashore, and asked him what he went away out there for. He said he could not understand me. I repeated. Still he could not understand. He appeared to be very ignorant of French. The doctor tried him, but he could not understand the doctor. I asked this boatman to explain his conduct, which he did; and then I couldn't understand *him*. Dan said:

'Oh, go to the pier, you old fool – that's where we want to go!'

We reasoned calmly with Dan that it was useless to speak to this foreigner in English – that he had better let us conduct this business in the French language and not let the stranger see how uncultivated he was.

'Well, go on, go on,' he said, 'don't mind me. I don't wish to interfere. Only, if you go on telling him in your kind of French, he never will find out where we want to go to. That is what I think about it.'

We rebuked him severely for this remark and said we never knew an ignorant person yet but was prejudiced. The Frenchman spoke again, and the doctor said:

'There now, Dan, he says he is going to allez to the douain. Means he is going to the hotel. Oh, certainly – we don't know the French language.'

This was a crusher, as Jack would say. It silenced further criticism from the disaffected member. We coasted past the sharp bows of a navy of great steamships and stopped at last at a government building on a stone pier. It was easy to remember then that the douane was the customhouse and not the hotel. We did not mention it, however. With winning French politeness the officers merely opened and closed our satchels, declined to examine our passports, and sent us on our way. We stopped at the first cafe we came to and entered. An old woman seated us at a table and waited for orders.

The doctor said: 'Avez-vous du vin?'

The dame looked perplexed. The doctor said again, with elaborate distinctness of articulation:

'Avez-vous du – vin!'

The dame looked more perplexed than before. I said:

'Doctor, there is a flaw in your pronunciation somewhere. Let me try her. Madame, avez-vous du vin? – It isn't any use, Doctor – take the witness.'

'Madame, avez-vous du vin – du fromage – pain – pickled pigs' feet – beurre – des oeufs – du boeuf – horseradish, sauerkraut, hog and hominy – anything, *anything* in the world that can stay a Christian stomach!'

She said:

'Bless you, why didn't you speak English before? I don't know anything about your plagued French!'

The humiliating taunts of the disaffected member spoiled the supper, and we dispatched it in angry silence and got away as soon as we could. Here we were in beautiful France – in a vast stone house of quaint architecture – surrounded by all manner of curiously worded French signs – stared at by strangely habited, bearded French people – everything gradually and surely forcing upon us the coveted consciousness that at last, and beyond all question, we *were* in beautiful France and absorbing its nature to the forgetfulness of everything else, and coming to feel the happy romance of the thing in all its enchanting delightfulness – and to think of this skinny veteran intruding with her vile English, at such a moment, to blow the fair vision to the winds! It was exasperating.

We set out to find the center of the city, inquiring the direction every now and then. We never did succeed in making anybody understand just exactly what we wanted, and neither did we ever succeed in comprehending just exactly what they said in reply, but then they always pointed – they always did that – and we bowed politely and said, 'Merci, monsieur', and so it was a blighting triumph over the disaffected member anyway. He was restive under these victories and often asked:

'What did that pirate say?'

'Why, he told us which way to go to find the Grand Casino.'

'Yes, but what did he *say*?'

'Oh, it don't matter what he said – *we* understood him. These are educated people – not like that absurd boatman.'

'Well, I wish they were educated enough to tell a man a direction that goes *somewhere* – for we've been going around in a circle for an hour. I've passed this same old drugstore seven times.'

We said it was a low, disreputable falsehood (but we knew it was not). It was plain that it would not do to pass that drugstore again, though – we might go on asking directions, but we must cease from following finger-pointings if we hoped to check the suspicions of the disaffected member.

A long walk through smooth, asphaltum-paved streets bordered by blocks of vast new mercantile houses of cream-colored stone every house and every block precisely like all the other houses and all the other blocks for a mile, and all brilliantly lighted – brought us at last to the principal thoroughfare. On every hand were bright colors, flashing constellations of gas burners, gaily dressed men and women thronging the sidewalks – hurry, life, activity, cheerfulness, conversation, and laughter everywhere! We found the Grand Hotel du Louvre et de la Paix, and wrote down who we were, where we were born, what our occupations were, the place we came from last, whether we were married or single, how we liked it, how old we were, where we were bound for and when we expected to get there, and a great deal of information of similar importance – all for the benefit of the landlord and the secret police. We hired a guide and began the business of sightseeing immediately. That first night on French soil was a stirring one. I cannot think of half the places we went to or what we particularly saw; we had no disposition to examine carefully into anything at all – we only wanted to glance and go – to move, keep moving! The spirit of the country was upon us. We sat down, finally, at a late hour, in the great Casino, and called for unstinted champagne. It is so easy to be bloated aristocrats where it costs nothing of consequence! There were about 500 people in that dazzling place, I suppose, though the walls being papered entirely with mirrors, so to speak, one could not really tell but that there were a hundred thousand. Young, daintily dressed exquisites and young, stylishly dressed women, and also old gentlemen and old ladies, sat in couples and groups about innumerable marble-topped tables and ate fancy suppers, drank wine, and kept up a chattering din of conversation that was dazing to the senses. There was a stage at the far end and a large orchestra; and every now and then actors and actresses in preposterous comic dresses came out and sang the most extravagantly funny songs, to judge by their absurd actions; but that audience merely suspended its chatter, stared cynically, and never once smiled, never once applauded! I had always thought that Frenchmen were ready to laugh at anything.

⋯❦⋯

We are getting foreignized rapidly and with facility. We are getting reconciled to halls and bedchambers with unhomelike stone floors and no carpets – floors that ring to the tread of one's heels with a sharpness that is death to sentimental musing. We are getting used to tidy, noiseless waiters, who glide hither and thither, and hover about your back and your elbows like butterflies, quick to comprehend orders, quick to fill them; thankful for a gratuity without regard to the amount; and always polite – never otherwise than polite. That is the strangest curiosity yet – a really polite hotel waiter who isn't an idiot. We are getting used to driving right into the central court of the hotel, in the midst of a fragrant circle of vines and flowers, and in the midst also of parties of gentlemen sitting quietly reading the paper and smoking. We are getting used to ice frozen by artificial process in ordinary bottles – the only kind of ice they have here. We are getting used to all these things, but we are *not* getting used to carrying our own soap. We are sufficiently civilized to carry our own combs and toothbrushes, but this thing of having to ring for soap every time we wash is new to us and not pleasant at all. We think of it just after we get our heads and faces thoroughly wet or just when we think we have been in the bathtub long enough, and then, of course, an annoying delay follows. These Marseillais make Marseillaise hymns and Marseilles vests and Marseilles soap for all the world, but they never sing their hymns or wear their vests or wash with their soap themselves.

We have learned to go through the lingering routine of the table d'hôte[1] with patience, with serenity, with satisfaction. We take soup, then wait a few minutes for the fish; a few minutes more and the plates are changed, and the roast beef comes; another change and we take peas; change again and take lentils; change and take snail patties (I prefer grasshoppers); change and take roast chicken and salad; then strawberry pie and ice cream; then green figs, pears, oranges, green almonds, etc.; finally coffee. Wine with every course, of course, being in France. With such a cargo on board, digestion is a slow process, and we must sit long in the cool chambers and smoke – and read French newspapers, which have a strange fashion of telling a perfectly straight story till you get to the 'nub' of it, and then a word drops in that no man can translate, and that story is ruined. An embankment fell on some Frenchmen yesterday, and the papers are full of it today – but whether those sufferers were killed, or crippled, or bruised, or only scared is more than I can possibly make out, and yet I would just give anything to know.

We were troubled a little at dinner today by the conduct of an American, who talked very loudly and coarsely and laughed boisterously where all others were so quiet and well behaved. He ordered wine with a royal flourish and said:

'I never dine without wine, sir,' (which was a pitiful falsehood), and looked around upon the company to bask in the admiration he expected to find in their faces. All these airs in a land where they would as soon expect to leave the soup out of the bill of fare as the wine! – in a land where wine is nearly as common among all ranks as water! This fellow said: 'I am a free-born sovereign, sir, an American, sir, and I want everybody to know it!' He did not mention that he was a lineal descendant of Balaam's ass, but everybody knew that without his telling it.

We have driven in the Prado – that superb avenue bordered with patrician mansions and noble shade trees – and have visited the Chateau Boarely and its curious museum. They showed us a miniature cemetery there – a copy of the first graveyard that was ever in Marseilles, no doubt. The delicate little skeletons were lying in broken vaults and had their household gods and kitchen utensils with them. The original of this cemetery was dug up in the principal street of the city a few years ago. It had remained there, only twelve feet underground, for a matter of 2,500 years or thereabouts. Romulus was here before he built Rome, and thought something of founding a city on this spot, but gave up the idea. He may have been personally acquainted with some of these Phoenicians whose skeletons we have been examining.

In the great Zoological Gardens we found specimens of all the animals the world produces, I think, including a dromedary, a monkey ornamented with tufts of brilliant blue and carmine hair – a very gorgeous monkey he was – a hippopotamus from the Nile, and a sort of tall, long-legged bird with a beak like a powder horn and close-fitting wings like the tails of a dress coat. This fellow stood up with his eyes shut and his shoulders stooped forward a little, and looked as if he had his hands under his coat tails. Such tranquil stupidity, such supernatural gravity, such self-righteousness, and such ineffable self-complacency as were in the countenance and attitude of that gray-bodied, dark-winged, bald-headed, and preposterously uncomely bird! He was so ungainly, so pimply about the head, so scaly about the legs, yet so serene, so unspeakably satisfied! He was the most comical-looking creature that can be imagined.

It was good to hear Dan and the doctor laugh – such natural and such enjoyable laughter had not been heard among our excursionists since our ship sailed away from America. This bird was a godsend to us, and I should be an ingrate if I forgot to make honorable mention of him in these pages. Ours was a pleasure excursion; therefore we stayed with that bird an hour and made the most of him. We stirred him up occasionally, but he only unclosed an eye and slowly closed it again, abating no jot of his stately piety of demeanor or his tremendous seriousness. He only seemed to say, 'Defile not Heaven's anointed with unsanctified hands.' We did not know his name, and so we called him 'The Pilgrim'. Dan said:

'All he wants now is a Plymouth Collection.'

The boon companion of the colossal elephant was a common cat! This cat had a fashion of climbing up the elephant's hind legs and roosting on his back. She would sit up there, with her paws curved under her breast, and sleep in the sun half the afternoon. It used to annoy the elephant at first, and he would reach up and take her down, but she would go aft and climb up again. She persisted until she finally conquered the elephant's prejudices, and now they are inseparable friends. The cat plays about her comrade's forefeet or his trunk often, until dogs approach, and then she goes aloft out of danger. The elephant has annihilated several dogs lately that pressed his companion too closely.

We hired a sailboat and a guide and made an excursion to one of the small islands in the harbor to visit the Castle d'If. This ancient fortress has a melancholy history. It has been used as a prison for political offenders for 200 or 300 years, and its dungeon walls are scarred with the rudely carved names of many and many a captive who fretted his life away here and left no record of himself but these sad epitaphs wrought with his own hands. How thick the names were! And their long-departed owners seemed to throng the gloomy cells and corridors with their phantom shapes. We loitered through dungeon after dungeon, away down into the living rock below the level of the sea, it seemed. Names everywhere! – some plebeian, some noble, some even princely. Plebeian, prince, and noble had one solicitude in common – they would not be forgotten! They could suffer solitude, inactivity, and the horrors of a silence that no sound ever disturbed, but they could not bear the thought of being utterly forgotten by the world. Hence the carved names. In one cell, where a little light penetrated, a man had lived twenty-seven years without seeing the face of a human being – lived in filth and wretchedness, with no companionship but his own thoughts, and they were sorrowful enough and hopeless enough, no doubt. Whatever his jailers considered that he needed was conveyed to his cell by night through a wicket.

This man carved the walls of his prison house from floor to roof with all manner of figures of men and animals grouped in intricate designs. He had toiled there year after year, at his self-appointed task, while infants grew to boyhood – to vigorous youth – idled through school and college – acquired a profession – claimed man's mature estate – married and looked back to infancy as to a thing of some vague, ancient time, almost. But who shall tell how many ages it seemed to this prisoner? With the one, time flew sometimes; with the other, never – it crawled always. To the one, nights spent in dancing had seemed made of minutes instead of hours; to the other, those selfsame nights had been like all other nights of dungcon life and seemed made of slow, dragging weeks instead of hours and minutes.

One prisoner of fifteen years had scratched verses upon his walls, and brief prose sentences – brief, but full of pathos. These spoke not of himself and his hard estate, but only of the shrine where his spirit fled the prison to worship – of home and the idols that were templed there. He never lived to see them.

The walls of these dungeons are as thick as some bedchambers at home are wide – fifteen feet. We saw the damp, dismal cells in which two of Dumas' heroes passed their confinement – heroes of 'Monte Cristo'. It was here that the brave Abbé wrote a book with his own blood, with a pen made of a piece of iron hoop, and by the light of a lamp made out of shreds of cloth soaked in grease obtained from his food; and then dug through the thick wall with some trifling instrument which he wrought himself out of a stray piece of iron or table cutlery and freed Dantes from his chains. It was a pity that so many weeks of dreary labor should have come to naught at last.

They showed us the noisome cell where the celebrated 'Iron Mask' – that ill-starred brother of a hardhearted king of France – was confined for a season before he was sent to hide the strange mystery of his life from the curious in the dungeons of Sainte Marguerite. The place had a far greater interest for us than it could have had if we had known beyond all question who the Iron Mask was, and what his history had been, and why this most unusual punishment had been meted out to him. Mystery! That was the charm. That speechless tongue, those prisoned features, that heart so freighted with unspoken troubles, and that breast so oppressed with its piteous secret had been here. These dank walls had known the man whose dolorous story is a sealed book forever! There was fascination in the spot.

❦

We have come 500 miles by rail through the heart of France. What a bewitching land it is! What a garden! Surely the leagues of bright green lawns are swept and brushed and watered every day and their grasses trimmed by the barber. Surely the hedges are shaped and measured and their symmetry preserved by the most architectural of gardeners. Surely the long straight rows of stately poplars that divide the beautiful landscape like the squares of a checker-board are set with line and plummet, and their uniform height determined with a spirit level. Surely the straight, smooth, pure white turnpikes are jack-planed and sandpapered every day. How else are these marvels of symmetry, cleanliness, and order attained? It is wonderful. There are no unsightly stone walls and never a fence of any kind. There is no dirt, no decay, no rubbish anywhere – nothing that even hints at untidiness – nothing that ever suggests neglect. All is orderly and beautiful – everything is charming to the eye.

We had such glimpses of the Rhone gliding along between its grassy banks; of cosy cottages buried in flowers and shrubbery; of quaint old red-tiled villages with mossy medieval cathedrals looming out of their midst; of wooded hills with ivy-grown towers and turrets of feudal castles projecting above the foliage; such glimpses of Paradise, it seemed to us, such visions of fabled fairyland!

We knew then what the poet meant when he sang of: '– thy cornfields green, and sunny vines, O pleasant land of France!'

And it *is* a pleasant land. No word describes it so felicitously as that one. They say there is no word for 'home' in the French language. Well, considering that they have the article itself in such an attractive aspect, they ought to manage to get along without the word. Let us not waste too much pity on 'homeless' France. I have observed that Frenchmen abroad seldom wholly give up the idea of going back to France some time or other. I am not surprised at it now.

We are not infatuated with these French railway cars, though. We took first-class passage, not because we wished to attract attention by doing a thing which is uncommon in Europe but because we could make our journey quicker by so doing. It is hard to make railroading pleasant in any country. It is too tedious. Stagecoaching is infinitely more delightful. Once I crossed the plains and deserts and mountains of the West in a stagecoach, from the Missouri line to California, and since then all my pleasure trips must be measured to that rare holiday frolic. Two thousand miles of ceaseless rush and rattle and clatter, by night and by day, and never a weary moment, never a lapse of interest! The first 700 miles a level continent, its grassy carpet greener and softer and smoother than any sea and figured with designs fitted to its magnitude – the shadows of the clouds. Here were no scenes but summer scenes, and no disposition inspired by them but to lie at full length on the mail sacks in the grateful breeze and dreamily smoke the pipe of peace – what other, where all was repose and contentment? In cool mornings, before the sun was fairly up, it was worth a lifetime of city toiling and moiling to perch in the foretop with the driver and see the six mustangs scamper under the sharp snapping of the whip that never touched them; to scan the blue distances of a world that knew no lords but us; to cleave the wind with uncovered head and feel the sluggish pulses rousing to the spirit of a speed that pretended to the resistless rush of a typhoon! Then 1,300 miles of desert solitudes; of limitless panoramas of bewildering perspective; of mimic cities, of pinnacled cathedrals, of massive fortresses, counterfeited in the eternal rocks and splendid with the crimson and gold of the setting sun; of dizzy altitudes among fog-wreathed peaks and never-melting snows, where thunders and lightnings and tempests warred magnificently at our feet and the storm clouds above swung their shredded banners in our very faces! But I forgot. I am in elegant France now, and not scurrying through the great South Pass and the Wind River Mountains, among antelopes and buffaloes and painted Indians on the warpath. It is not meet that I should make too disparaging comparisons between humdrum travel on a railway and that royal summer flight across a continent in a stagecoach. I meant in the beginning to say that railway journeying is tedious and tiresome, and so it is – though at the time I was thinking particularly of a dismal fifty-hour pilgrimage between New York and St Louis. Of course our trip through France was not really tedious because all its scenes and experiences were new and strange; but as Dan says, it had its 'discrepancies'.

The cars are built in compartments that hold eight persons each. Each compartment is partially subdivided, and so there are two tolerably distinct parties of four in it. Four face the other four. The seats and backs are thickly padded and cushioned and are very comfortable; you can smoke if you wish; there are no bothersome peddlers; you are saved the infliction of a multitude of disagreeable fellow passengers. So far, so well. But then the conductor locks you in when the train starts; there is no water to drink in the car; there is no heating apparatus for night travel; if a drunken rowdy should get in, you could not remove a matter of twenty seats from him or enter another car; but above all, if you are worn out and must sleep, you must sit up and do it in naps, with cramped legs and in a torturing misery that leaves you withered and lifeless the next day – for behold they have not that culmination of all charity and human kindness, a sleeping car, in all France. I prefer the American system. It has not so many grievous 'discrepancies'.

In France, all is clockwork, all is order. They make no mistakes. Every third man wears a uniform, and whether he be a marshal of the empire or a brakeman, he is ready and perfectly willing to answer all your questions with tireless politeness, ready to tell you which car to take, yea, and ready to go and put you into it to make sure that you shall not go astray. You cannot pass into the waiting room of the depot till you have secured your ticket, and you cannot pass from its only exit till the train is at its threshold to receive you. Once on board, the train will not start till your ticket has been examined – till every passenger's ticket has been inspected. This is chiefly for your own good. If by any possibility you have managed to take the wrong train, you will be handed over to a polite official who will take you whither you belong and bestow you with many an affable bow. Your ticket will be inspected every now and then along the route, and when it is time to change cars you will know it. You are in the hands of officials who zealously study your welfare and your interest, instead of turning their talents to the invention of new methods of discommoding and snubbing you, as is very often the main employment of that exceedingly self-satisfied monarch, the railroad conductor of America.

But the happiest regulation in French railway government is – thirty minutes to dinner! No five-minute boltings of flabby rolls, muddy coffee, questionable eggs, gutta-percha beef, and pies whose conception and execution are a dark and bloody mystery to all save the cook that created them!

No, we sat calmly down – it was in old Dijon, which is so easy to spell and so impossible to pronounce except when you civilize it and call it Demijohn – and poured out rich Burgundian wines and munched calmly through a long table d'hôte bill of fare, snail patties, delicious fruits and all, then paid the trifle it cost and stepped happily aboard the train again, without once cursing the railroad company. A rare experience and one to be treasured forever.

They say they do not have accidents on these French roads, and I think it must be true. If I remember rightly, we passed high above wagon roads or through tunnels under them, but never crossed them on their own level. About every quarter of a mile, it seemed to me, a man came out and held up a club till the train went by, to signify that everything was safe ahead. Switches were changed a mile in advance by pulling a wire rope that passed along the ground by the rail, from station to station. Signals for the day and signals for the night gave constant and timely notice of the position of switches.

No, they have no railroad accidents to speak of in France. But why? Because when one occurs, *somebody* has to hang for it! Not hang, maybe, but be punished at least with such vigor of emphasis as to make negligence a thing to be shuddered at by railroad officials for many a day thereafter. 'No blame attached to the officers' – that lying and disaster-breeding verdict so common to our softhearted juries is seldom rendered in France. If the trouble occurred in the conductor's department, that officer must suffer if his subordinate cannot be proven guilty; if in the engineer's department and the case be similar, the engineer must answer.

The Old Travelers – those delightful parrots who have 'been here before' and know more about the country than Louis Napoleon knows now or ever will know – tell us these things, and we believe them because they are pleasant things to believe and because they are plausible and savor of the rigid subjection to law and order which we behold about us everywhere.

But we love the Old Travelers. We love to hear them prate and drivel and lie. We can tell them the moment we see them. They always throw out a few feelers; they never cast themselves adrift till they have sounded every individual and know that he has not traveled. Then they open their throttle valves, and how they do brag, and sneer, and swell, and soar, and blaspheme the sacred name of Truth! Their central idea, their grand aim, is to subjugate you, keep you down, make you feel insignificant and humble in the blaze of their cosmopolitan glory! They will not let you know anything. They sneer at your most inoffensive suggestions; they laugh unfeelingly at your treasured dreams of foreign lands; they brand the statements of your traveled aunts and uncles as the stupidest absurdities; they deride your most trusted authors and demolish the fair images they have set up for your willing worship with the pitiless ferocity of the fanatic iconoclast! But still I love the Old Travelers. I love them for their witless platitudes, for their supernatural ability to bore, for their delightful asinine vanity, for their luxuriant fertility of imagination, for their startling, their brilliant, their overwhelming mendacity!

By Lyons and the Saone (where we saw the lady of Lyons and thought little of her comeliness), by Villa Franca, Tonnere, venerable Sens, Melun, Fontainebleau, and scores of other beautiful cities, we swept, always noting the absence of hog-wallows, broken fences, cow lots, unpainted houses, and mud, and always noting, as well, the presence of cleanliness, grace, taste in adorning and beautifying, even to the disposition of a tree or the turning of a hedge, the marvel of roads in perfect repair, void of ruts and guiltless of even an inequality of surface – we bowled along, hour after hour, that brilliant summer day, and as nightfall approached we entered a wilderness of odorous flowers and shrubbery, sped through it, and then, excited, delighted, and half persuaded that we were only the sport of a beautiful dream, lo, we stood in magnificent Paris!

What excellent order they kept about that vast depot! There was no frantic crowding and jostling, no shouting and swearing, and no swaggering intrusion of services by rowdy hackmen. These latter gentry stood outside – stood quietly by their long line of vehicles and said never a word. A kind of hackman general seemed to have the whole matter of transportation in his hands. He politely received the passengers and ushered them to the kind of conveyance they wanted, and told the driver where to deliver them. There was no 'talking back', no dissatisfaction about overcharging, no grumbling about anything. In a little while we were speeding through the streets of Paris and delightfully recognizing certain names and places with which books had long ago made us familiar. It was like meeting an old friend when we read Rue de Rivoli on the street corner; we knew the genuine vast palace of the Louvre as well as we knew its picture; when we passed by the Column of July we needed no one to tell us what it was or to remind us that on its site once stood the grim Bastille, that grave of human hopes and happiness, that dismal prison house within whose dungeons so many young faces put on the wrinkles of age, so many proud spirits grew humble, so many brave hearts broke.

We secured rooms at the hotel, or rather, we had three beds put into one room, so that we might be together, and then we went out to a restaurant, just after lamplighting, and ate a comfortable, satisfactory, lingering dinner. It was a pleasure to eat where everything was so tidy, the food so well cooked, the waiters so polite, and the coming and departing company so moustached, so frisky, so affable, so fearfully and wonderfully Frenchy! All the surroundings were gay and enlivening. Two hundred people sat at little tables on the sidewalk, sipping wine and coffee; the streets were thronged with light vehicles and with joyous pleasure-seekers; there was music in the air, life and action all about us, and a conflagration of gaslight everywhere!

After dinner we felt like seeing such Parisian specialties as we might see without distressing exertion, and so we sauntered through the brilliant streets and looked at the dainty trifles in variety stores and jewelry shops. Occasionally, merely for the pleasure of being cruel, we put unoffending Frenchmen on the rack with questions framed in the incomprehensible jargon of their native language, and while they writhed we impaled them, we peppered them, we scarified them, with their own vile verbs and participles.

We noticed that in the jewelry stores they had some of the articles marked 'gold' and some labeled 'imitation'. We wondered at this extravagance of honesty and inquired into the matter. We were informed that inasmuch as most people are not able to tell false gold from the genuine article, the government compels jewelers to have their gold work assayed and stamped officially according to its fineness and their imitation work duly labeled with the sign of its falsity. They told us the jewelers would not dare to violate this law, and that whatever a stranger bought in one of their stores might be depended upon as being strictly what it was represented to be. Verily, a wonderful land is France!

Then we hunted for a barbershop. From earliest infancy it had been a cherished ambition of mine to be shaved some day in a palatial barbershop in Paris. I wished to recline at full length in a cushioned invalid chair, with pictures about me and sumptuous furniture; with frescoed walls and gilded arches above me and vistas of Corinthian columns stretching far before me; with perfumes of Araby to intoxicate my senses and the slumberous drone of distant noises to soothe me to sleep. At the end of an hour I would wake up regretfully and find my face as smooth and as soft as an infant's. Departing, I would lift my hands above that barber's head and say, 'Heaven bless you, my son!'

So we searched high and low, for a matter of two hours, but never a barbershop could we see. We saw only wig-making establishments, with shocks of dead and repulsive hair bound upon the heads of painted waxen brigands who stared out from glass boxes upon the passer-by with their stony eyes and scared him with the ghostly white of their countenances. We shunned these signs for a time, but finally we concluded that the wig-makers must of necessity be the barbers as well, since we could find no single legitimate representative of the fraternity. We entered and asked, and found that it was even so.

I said I wanted to be shaved. The barber inquired where my room was. I said never mind where my room was, I wanted to be shaved – there, on the spot. The doctor said he would be shaved also. Then there was an excitement among those two barbers! There was a wild consultation, and afterwards a hurrying to and fro and a feverish gathering up of razors from obscure places and a ransacking for soap. Next they took us into a little mean, shabby back room; they got two ordinary sitting-room chairs and placed us in them with our coats on. My old, old dream of bliss vanished into thin air!

I sat bolt upright, silent, sad and solemn. One of the wig-making villains lathered my face for ten terrible minutes and finished by plastering a mass of suds into my mouth. I expelled the nasty stuff with a strong English expletive and said, 'Foreigner, beware!' Then this outlaw strapped his razor on his boot, hovered over me ominously for six fearful seconds, and then swooped down upon me like the genius of destruction. The first rake of his razor loosened the very hide from my face and lifted me out of the chair. I stormed and raved, and the other boys enjoyed it. Their beards are not strong and thick. Let us draw the curtain over this harrowing scene.

Suffice it that I submitted and went through with the cruel infliction of a shave by a French barber; tears of exquisite agony coursed down my cheeks now and then, but I survived. Then the incipient assassin held a basin of water under my chin and slopped its contents over my face, and into my bosom, and down the back of my neck, with a mean pretense of washing away the soap and blood. He dried my features with a towel and was going to comb my hair, but I asked to be excused. I said, with withering irony, that it was sufficient to be skinned – I declined to be scalped.

I went away from there with my handkerchief about my face, and never, never, never desired to dream of palatial Parisian barbershops anymore. The truth is, as I believe I have since found out, that they have no barbershops worthy of the name in Paris – and no barbers, either, for that matter. The impostor who does duty as a barber brings his pans and napkins and implements of torture to your residence and deliberately skins you in your private apartments. Ah, I have suffered, suffered, suffered, here in Paris, but never mind – the time is coming when I shall have a dark and bloody revenge. Someday a Parisian barber will come to my room to skin me, and from that day forth that barber will never be heard of more.

At eleven o'clock we alighted upon a sign which manifestly referred to billiards. Joy! We had played billiards in the Azores with balls that were not round and on an ancient table that was very little smoother than a brick pavement – one of those wretched old things with dead cushions, and with patches in the faded cloth and invisible obstructions that made the balls describe the most astonishing and unsuspected angles and perform feats in the way of unlooked-for and almost impossible 'scratches' that were perfectly bewildering. We had played at Gibraltar with balls the size of a walnut, on a table like a public square – and in both instances we achieved far more aggravation than amusement. We expected to fare better here, but we were mistaken. The cushions were a good deal higher than the balls, and as the balls had a fashion of always stopping under the cushions, we accomplished very little in the way of caroms. The cushions were hard and unelastic, and the cues were so crooked that in making a shot you had to allow for the curve or you would infallibly put the 'English' on the wrong side of the ball. Dan was to mark while the doctor and I played. At the end of an hour neither of us had made a count, and so Dan was tired of keeping tally with nothing to tally, and we were heated and angry and disgusted. We paid the heavy bill – about six cents – and said we would call around sometime when we had a week to spend, and finish the game.

We adjourned to one of those pretty cafes and took supper and tested the wines of the country, as we had been instructed to do, and found them harmless and unexciting. They might have been exciting, however, if we had chosen to drink a sufficiency of them.

To close our first day in Paris cheerfully and pleasantly, we now sought our grand room in the Grand Hotel du Louvre and climbed into our sumptuous bed to read and smoke – but alas!

It was pitiful,
In a whole city-full,
Gas we had none.
(Joke by the Doctor)

No gas to read by – nothing but dismal candles. It was a shame. We tried to map out excursions for the morrow; we puzzled over French 'guides to Paris'; we talked disjointedly in a vain endeavor to make head or tail of the wild chaos of the day's sights and experiences; we subsided to indolent smoking; we gaped and yawned and stretched – then feebly wondered if we were really and truly in renowned Paris, and drifted drowsily away into that vast mysterious void which men call sleep.

❧

The next morning we were up and dressed at ten o'clock. We went to the 'commissionaire' of the hotel – I don't know what a 'commissionaire' is, but that is the man we went to – and told him we wanted a guide. He said the national Exposition had drawn such multitudes of Englishmen and Americans to Paris that it would be next to impossible to find a good guide unemployed. He said he usually kept a dozen or two on hand, but he only had three now.

He called them. One looked so like a very pirate that we let him go at once. The next one spoke with a simpering precision of pronunciation that was irritating and said:

'If ze zhentlemans will to me make ze grande honneur to me rattain in hees serveece, I shall show to him every sing zat is magnifique to look upon in ze beautiful Parree. I speaky ze Angleesh pairfaitemaw.'

He would have done well to have stopped there, because he had that much by heart and said it right off without making a mistake. But his self-complacency seduced him into attempting a flight into regions of unexplored English, and the reckless experiment was his ruin. Within ten seconds he was so tangled up in a maze of mutilated verbs and torn and bleeding forms of speech that no human ingenuity could ever have gotten him out of it with credit. It was plain enough that he could not 'speaky' the English quite as 'pairfaitemaw' as he had pretended he could.

The third man captured us. He was plainly dressed, but he had a noticeable air of neatness about him. He wore a high silk hat which was a little old, but had been carefully brushed. He wore second-hand kid gloves, in good repair, and carried a small rattan cane with a curved handle – a female leg – of ivory. He stepped as gently and as daintily as a cat crossing a muddy street; and oh, he was urbanity; he was quiet, unobtrusive self-possession; he was deference itself! He spoke softly and guardedly; and when he was about to make a statement on his sole responsibility or offer a suggestion, he weighed it by drachms and scruples first, with the crook of his little stick placed meditatively to his teeth. His opening speech was perfect. It was perfect in construction, in phraseology, in grammar, in emphasis, in pronunciation – everything. He spoke little and guardedly after that. We were charmed. We were more than charmed – we were overjoyed. We hired him at once. We never even asked him his price. This man – our lackey, our servant, our unquestioning slave though he was – was still a gentleman – we could see that – while of the other two one was coarse and awkward and the other was a born pirate. We asked our man Friday's name. He drew from his pocketbook a snowy little card and passed it to us with a profound bow:

A. BILLFINGER,
—◇—

GUIDE TO PARIS,

France, Germany, Spain, etc., etc.,
Grand Hotel du Louvre.

'Billfinger! Oh, carry me home to die!'

That was an 'aside' from Dan. The atrocious name grated harshly on my ear, too. The most of us can learn to forgive, and even to like, a countenance that strikes us unpleasantly at first, but few of us, I fancy, become reconciled to a jarring name so easily. I was almost sorry we had hired this man, his name was so unbearable. However, no matter. We were impatient to start. Billfinger stepped to the door to call a carriage, and then the doctor said:

'Well, the guide goes with the barbershop, with the billiard-table, with the gasless room, and may be with many another pretty romance of Paris. I expected to have a guide named Henri de Montmorency, or Armand de la Chartreuse, or something that would sound grand in letters to the villagers at home, but to think of a Frenchman by the name of Billfinger! Oh! This is absurd, you know. This will never do. We can't say Billfinger; it is nauseating. Name him over again; what had we better call him? Alexis du Caulaincourt?'

'Alphonse Henri Gustave de Hauteville,' I suggested.

'Call him Ferguson,' said Dan.

That was practical, unromantic good sense. Without debate, we expunged Billfinger *as* Billfinger, and called him Ferguson.

The carriage – an open barouche – was ready. Ferguson mounted beside the driver, and we whirled away to breakfast. As was proper, Mr Ferguson stood by to transmit our orders and answer questions. By and by, he mentioned casually – the artful adventurer – that he would go and get his breakfast as soon as we had finished ours. He knew we could not get along without him and that we would not want to loiter about and wait for him. We asked him to sit down and eat with us. He begged, with many a bow, to be excused. It was not proper, he said; he would sit at another table. We ordered him peremptorily to sit down with us.

Here endeth the first lesson. It was a mistake.

As long as we had that fellow after that, he was always hungry; he was always thirsty. He came early; he stayed late; he could not pass a restaurant; he looked with a lecherous eye upon every wine shop. Suggestions to stop, excuses to eat and to drink, were forever on his lips. We tried all we could to fill him so full that he would have no room to spare for a fortnight, but it was a failure. He did not hold enough to smother the cravings of his superhuman appetite.

He had another 'discrepancy' about him. He was always wanting us to buy things. On the shallowest pretenses he would inveigle us into shirt stores, boot stores, tailor shops, glove shops – anywhere under the broad sweep of the heavens that there seemed a chance of our buying anything. Anyone could have guessed that the shopkeepers paid him a percentage on the sales, but in our blessed innocence we didn't until this feature of his conduct grew unbearably prominent. One day Dan happened to mention that he thought of buying three or four silk dress patterns for presents. Ferguson's hungry eye was upon him in an instant. In the course of twenty minutes the carriage stopped.

'What's this?'

'Zis is ze finest silk magazin in Paris – ze most celebrate.'

'What did you come here for? We told you to take us to the palace of the Louvre.'

'I suppose ze gentleman say he wish to buy some silk.'

'You are not required to "suppose" things for the party, Ferguson. We do not wish to tax your energies too much. We will bear some of the burden and heat of the day ourselves. We will endeavor to do such "supposing" as is really necessary to be done. Drive on.' So spake the doctor.

Within fifteen minutes the carriage halted again, and before another silk store. The doctor said:

'Ah, the palace of the Louvre – beautiful, beautiful edifice! Does the Emperor Napoleon live here now, Ferguson?'

'Ah, Doctor! You do jest; zis is not ze palace; we come there directly. But since we pass right by zis store, where is such beautiful silk –'

'Ah! I see, I see. I meant to have told you that we did not wish to purchase any silks today, but in my absent-mindedness I forgot it. I also meant to tell you we wished to go directly to the Louvre, but I forgot that also. However, we will go there now. Pardon my seeming carelessness, Ferguson. Drive on.'

Within the half hour we stopped again – in front of another silk store. We were angry; but the doctor was always serene, always smooth-voiced. He said:

'At last! How imposing the Louvre is, and yet how small! How exquisitely fashioned! How charmingly situated! – Venerable, venerable pile –'

'Pardon, Doctor, zis is not ze Louvre – it is –'

'What is it?'

'I have ze idea – it come to me in a moment – zat ze silk in zis magazine –'

'Ferguson, how heedless I am, I fully intended to tell you that we did not wish to buy any silks today, and I also intended to tell you that we yearned to go immediately to the palace of the Louvre, but enjoying the happiness of seeing you devour four breakfasts this morning has so filled me with pleasurable emotions that I neglect the commonest interests of the time. However, we will proceed now to the Louvre, Ferguson.'

'But, doctor,' (excitedly,) 'it will take not a minute – not but one small minute! Ze gentleman need not to buy if he not wish to – but only *look* at ze silk – *look* at ze beautiful fabric. [Then pleadingly.] *Sair* – just only one *leetle* moment!'

Dan said, 'Confound the idiot! I don't want to see any silks today, and I *won't* look at them. Drive on.'

And the doctor: 'We need no silks now, Ferguson. Our hearts yearn for the Louvre. Let us journey on – let us journey on.'

'But *doctor*! It is only one moment – one leetle moment. And ze time will be save – entirely save! Because zere is nothing to see now – it is too late. It want ten minute to four and ze Louvre close at four – *only* one leetle moment, Doctor!'

The treacherous miscreant! After four breakfasts and a gallon of champagne, to serve us such a scurvy trick. We got no sight of the countless treasures of art in the Louvre galleries that day, and our only poor little satisfaction was in the reflection that Ferguson sold not a solitary silk dress pattern.

I am writing this chapter partly for the satisfaction of abusing that accomplished knave Billfinger, and partly to show whosoever shall read this how Americans fare at the hands of the Paris guides and what sort of people Paris guides are. It need not be supposed that we were a stupider or an easier prey than our countrymen generally are, for we were not. The guides deceive and defraud every American who goes to Paris for the first time and sees its sights alone or in company with others as little experienced as himself. I shall visit Paris again someday, and then let the guides beware! I shall go in my war paint – I shall carry my tomahawk along.

❦

I think we have lost but little time in Paris. We have gone to bed every night tired out. Of course we visited the renowned International Exposition. All the world did that. We went there on our third day in Paris – and we stayed there *nearly two hours*. That was our first and last visit. To tell the truth, we saw at a glance that one would have to spend weeks – yea, even months – in that monstrous establishment to get an intelligible idea of it. It was a wonderful show, but the moving masses of people of all nations we saw there were a still more wonderful show. I discovered that if I were to stay there a month, I should still find myself looking at the people instead of the inanimate objects on exhibition. I got a little interested in some curious old tapestries of the thirteenth century, but a party of Arabs came by, and their dusky faces and quaint costumes called my attention away at once. I watched a silver swan, which had a living grace about his movements and a living intelligence in his eyes – watched him swimming about as comfortably and as unconcernedly as if he had been born in a morass instead of a jeweler's shop – watched him seize a silver fish from under the water and hold up his head and go through all the customary and elaborate motions of swallowing it – but the moment it disappeared down his throat some tattooed South Sea Islanders approached and I yielded to their attractions.

Presently I found a revolving pistol several hundred years old which looked strangely like a modern Colt, but just then I heard that the Empress of the French was in another part of the building, and hastened away to see what she might look like. We heard martial music – we saw an unusual number of soldiers walking hurriedly about – there was a general movement among the people. We inquired what it was all about and learned that the Emperor of the French and the Sultan of Turkey were about to review 25,000 troops at the Arc de l'Etoile. We immediately departed. I had a greater anxiety to see these men than I could have had to see twenty expositions.

We drove away and took up a position in an open space opposite the American minister's house. A speculator bridged a couple of barrels with a board and we hired standing places on it. Presently there was a sound of distant music; in another minute a pillar of dust came moving slowly toward us; a moment more and then, with colors flying and a grand crash of military music, a gallant array of cavalrymen emerged from the dust and came down the street on a gentle trot. After them came a long line of artillery; then more cavalry, in splendid uniforms; and then their imperial majesties Napoleon III and Abdul Aziz. The vast concourse of people swung their hats and shouted – the windows and housetops in the wide vicinity burst into a snowstorm of waving handkerchiefs, and the wavers of the same mingled their cheers with those of the masses below. It was a stirring spectacle.

✧❦✧

In Paris we often saw in shop windows the sign 'English Spoken Here', just as one sees in the windows at home the sign 'Ici on parle francaise'[ii]. We always invaded these places at once – and invariably received the information, framed in faultless French, that the clerk who did the English for the establishment had just gone to dinner and would be back in an hour – would Monsieur buy something? We wondered why those parties happened to take their dinners at such erratic and extraordinary hours, for we never called at a time when an exemplary Christian would be in the least likely to be abroad on such an errand. The truth was, it was a base fraud – a snare to trap the unwary – chaff to catch fledglings with. They had no English-murdering clerk.

They trusted to the sign to inveigle foreigners into their lairs, and trusted to their own blandishments to keep them there till they bought something.

We ferreted out another French imposition – a frequent sign to this effect: '*All manner of american drinks artistically prepared here.*' We procured the services of a gentleman experienced in the nomenclature of the American bar, and moved upon the works of one of these impostors. A bowing, aproned Frenchman skipped forward and said:

'Que voulez les messieurs?' I do not know what 'Que voulez les messieurs?' means, but such was his remark.

Our general said, 'We will take a whiskey straight.'

[A stare from the Frenchman.]

'Well, if you don't know what that is, give us a champagne cocktail.'

[A stare and a shrug.]

'Well, then, give us a sherry cobbler.'

The Frenchman was checkmated. This was all Greek to him.

'Give us a brandy smash!'

The Frenchman began to back away, suspicious of the ominous vigor of the last order – began to back away, shrugging his shoulders and spreading his hands apologetically.

The General followed him up and gained a complete victory. The uneducated foreigner could not even furnish a Santa Cruz Punch, an Eye-Opener, a Stone-Fence or an Earthquake. It was plain that he was a wicked impostor.

Enough of Paris for the present. We have done our whole duty by it. We have seen the Tuileries, the Napoleon Column, the Madeleine, that wonder of wonders the tomb of Napoleon, all the great churches and museums, libraries, imperial palaces, and sculpture and picture galleries, the Pantheon, Jardin des Plantes, the opera, the circus, the legislative body, the billiard rooms, the barbers, the *grisettes*[iii] –

Ah, the *grisettes*! I had almost forgotten. They are another romantic fraud. They were (if you let the books of travel tell it) always so beautiful – so neat and trim, so graceful – so naive and trusting – so gentle, so winning – so faithful to their shop duties, so irresistible to buyers in their prattling importunity – so devoted to their poverty-stricken students of the Latin Quarter – so lighthearted and happy on their Sunday picnics in the suburbs – and oh, so charmingly, so delightfully immoral!

Stuff! For three or four days I was constantly saying:

'Quick, Ferguson! Is that a *grisette*?'

And he always said, 'No.'

He comprehended at last that I wanted to see a grisette. Then he showed me dozens of them. They were like nearly all the Frenchwomen I ever saw – homely. They had large hands, large feet, large mouths; they had pug noses as a general thing, and moustaches that not even good breeding could overlook; they combed their hair straight back without parting; they were ill-shaped, they were not winning, they were not graceful; I knew by their looks that they ate garlic and onions; and lastly and finally, to my thinking it would be base flattery to call them immoral.

Aroint[iv] thee, wench! I sorrow for the vagabond student of the Latin Quarter now, even more than formerly I envied him. Thus topples to earth another idol of my infancy.

We have seen everything, and tomorrow we go to Versailles. We shall see Paris only for a little while as we come back to take up our line of march for the ship, and so I may as well bid the beautiful city a regretful farewell. We shall travel many thousands of miles after we leave here and visit many great cities, but we shall find none so enchanting as this.

Some of our party have gone to England, intending to take a roundabout course and rejoin the vessel at Leghorn or Naples several weeks hence. We came near going to Geneva, but have concluded to return to Marseilles and go up through Italy from Genoa.

I will conclude this chapter with a remark that I am sincerely proud to be able to make – and glad, as well, that my comrades cordially endorse it, to wit: by far the handsomest women we have seen in France were born and reared in America.

I feel now like a man who has redeemed a failing reputation and shed luster upon a dimmed escutcheon, by a single just deed done at the eleventh hour.

Let the curtain fall, to slow music.

Italy

We had a pleasant journey of it seaward again. We found that for the three past nights our ship had been in a state of war. The first night the sailors of a British ship, being happy with grog, came down on the pier and challenged our sailors to a free fight. They accepted with alacrity, repaired to the pier, and gained – their share of a drawn battle. Several bruised and bloody members of both parties were carried off by the police and imprisoned until the following morning. The next night the British boys came again to renew the fight, but our men had had strict orders to remain on board and out of sight. They did so, and the besieging party grew noisy and more and more abusive as the fact became apparent (to them) that our men were afraid to come out. They went away finally with a closing burst of ridicule and offensive epithets. The third night they came again and were more obstreperous than ever. They swaggered up and down the almost deserted pier, and hurled curses, obscenity, and stinging sarcasms at our crew. It was more than human nature could bear. The executive officer ordered our men ashore – with instructions not to fight. They charged the British and gained a brilliant victory. I probably would not have mentioned this war had it ended differently. But I travel to learn, and I still remember that they picture no French defeats in the battle-galleries of Versailles.

It was like home to us to step on board the comfortable ship again and smoke and lounge about her breezy decks. And yet it was not altogether like home, either, because so many members of the family were away. We missed some pleasant faces which we would rather have found at dinner, and at night there were gaps in the euchre-parties which could not be satisfactorily filled.

'Moult' was in England, Jack in Switzerland, Charley in Spain. Blucher was gone, none could tell where. But we were at sea again, and we had the stars and the ocean to look at, and plenty of room to meditate in.

In due time the shores of Italy were sighted, and as we stood gazing from the decks, early in the bright summer morning, the stately city of Genoa rose up out of the sea and flung back the sunlight from her hundred palaces.

Here we rest for the present – or rather, here we have been trying to rest, for some little time, but we run about too much to accomplish a great deal in that line.

I would like to remain here. I had rather not go any further. There may be prettier women in Europe, but I doubt it. The population of Genoa is 120,000; two-thirds of these are women, I think, and at least two-thirds of the women are beautiful. They are as dressy and as tasteful and as graceful as they could possibly be without being angels. However, angels are not very dressy, I believe. At least the angels in pictures are not – they wear nothing but wings. But these Genoese women do look so charming. Most of the young demoiselles are robed in a cloud of white from head to foot, though many trick themselves out more elaborately. Nine-tenths of them wear nothing on their heads but a filmy sort of veil, which falls down their backs like a white mist. They are very fair, and many of them have blue eyes, but black and dreamy dark brown ones are met with oftenest.

The ladies and gentlemen of Genoa have a pleasant fashion of promenading in a large park on the top of a hill in the center of the city, from six till nine in the evening, and then eating ices in a neighboring garden an hour or two longer. We went to the park on Sunday evening. Two thousand persons were present, chiefly young ladies and gentlemen. The gentlemen were dressed in the very latest Paris fashions, and the robes of the ladies glinted among the trees like so many snowflakes. The multitude moved round and round the park in a great procession. The bands played, and so did the fountains; the moon and the gas lamps lit up the scene, and altogether it was a brilliant and an animated picture. I scanned every female face that passed, and it seemed to me that all were handsome. I never saw such a freshet of loveliness before. I did not see how a man of only ordinary decision of character could marry here, because before he could get his mind made up he would fall in love with somebody else.

Never smoke any Italian tobacco. Never do it on any account. It makes me shudder to think what it must be made of. You cannot throw an old cigar 'stub' down anywhere, but some vagabond will pounce upon it on the instant. I like to smoke a good deal, but it wounds my sensibilities to see one of these stub-hunters watching me out of the corners of his hungry eyes and calculating how long my cigar will be likely to last. It reminded me too painfully of that San Francisco undertaker who used to go to sickbeds with his watch in his hand and time the corpse. One of these stub-hunters followed us all over the park last night, and we never had a smoke that was worth anything. We were always moved to appease him with the stub before the cigar was half gone, because he looked so viciously anxious. He regarded us as his own legitimate prey, by right of discovery, I think, because he drove off several other professionals who wanted to take stock in us.

Now, they surely must chew up those old stubs, and dry and sell them for smoking-tobacco. Therefore, give your custom to other than Italian brands of the article.

'The Superb' and the 'City of Palaces' are names which Genoa has held for centuries. She is full of palaces, certainly, and the palaces are sumptuous inside, but they are very rusty without and make no pretensions to architectural magnificence. 'Genoa the Superb' would be a felicitous title if it referred to the women.

We have visited several of the palaces – immense thick-walled piles, with great stone staircases, tesselated marble pavements on the floors, (sometimes they make a mosaic work, of intricate designs, wrought in pebbles or little fragments of marble laid in cement,) and grand salons hung with pictures by Rubens, Guido, Titian, Paul Veronese, and so on, and portraits of heads of the family, in plumed helmets and gallant coats of mail, and patrician ladies in stunning costumes of centuries ago. But, of course, the folks were all out in the country for the summer, and might not have known enough to ask us to dinner if they had been at home, and so all the grand empty salons, with their resounding pavements, their grim pictures of dead ancestors, and tattered banners with the dust of bygone centuries upon them, seemed to brood solemnly of death and the grave, and our spirits ebbed away, and our cheerfulness passed from us. We never went up to the eleventh story. We always began to suspect ghosts. There was always an undertaker-looking servant along, too, who handed us a program, pointed to the picture that began the list of the salon he was in, and then stood stiff and stark and unsmiling in his petrified livery till we were ready to move on to the next chamber, whereupon he marched sadly ahead and took up another malignantly respectful position as before. I wasted so much time praying that the roof would fall in on these dispiriting flunkies that I had but little left to bestow upon palace and pictures.

And besides, as in Paris, we had a guide. Perdition catch all the guides. This one said he was the most gifted linguist in Genoa, as far as English was concerned, and that only two persons in the city beside himself could talk the language at all. He showed us the birthplace of Christopher Columbus, and after we had reflected in silent awe before it for fifteen minutes, he said it was not the birthplace of Columbus, but of Columbus' grandmother! When we demanded an explanation of his conduct he only shrugged his shoulders and answered in barbarous Italian. I shall speak further of this guide in a future chapter. All the information we got out of him we shall be able to carry along with us, I think.

'Do you wis zo haut can be?"

That was what the guide asked when we were looking up at the bronze horses on the Arch of Peace. It meant, do you wish to go up there? I give it as a specimen of guide-English. These are the people that make life a burthen to the tourist. Their tongues are never still. They talk forever and forever, and that is the kind of billingsgate they use. Inspiration itself could hardly comprehend them. If they would only show you a masterpiece of art, or a venerable tomb, or a prison-house, or a battle-field, hallowed by touching memories or historical reminiscences, or grand traditions, and then step aside and hold still for ten minutes and let you think, it would not be so bad. But they interrupt every dream, every pleasant train of thought, with their tiresome cackling. Sometimes when I have been standing before some cherished old idol of mine that I remembered years and years ago in pictures in the geography at school, I have thought I would give a whole world if the human parrot at my side would suddenly perish where he stood and leave me to gaze, and ponder, and worship.

No, we did not 'wis zo haut can be'. We wished to go to La Scala, the largest theater in the world, I think they call it. We did so. It was a large place. Seven separate and distinct masses of humanity – six great circles and a monster parquette.

We wished to go to the Ambrosian Library, and we did that also. We saw a manuscript of Virgil, with annotations in the handwriting of Petrarch, the gentleman who loved another man's Laura, and lavished upon her all through life a love which was a clear waste of the raw material. It was sound sentiment, but bad judgment. It brought both parties fame, and created a fountain of commiseration for them in sentimental breasts that is running yet. But who says a word in behalf of poor Mr Laura? (I do not know his other name.) Who glorifies him? Who bedews him with tears? Who writes poetry about him? Nobody. How do you suppose *he* liked the state of things that has given the world so much pleasure? How did he enjoy having another man following his wife everywhere and making her name a familiar word in every garlic-exterminating mouth in Italy with his sonnets to her pre-empted eyebrows? *They* got fame and sympathy – he got neither. This is a peculiarly felicitous instance of what is called poetical justice. It is all very fine; but it does not chime with my notions of right. It is too one-sided – too ungenerous.

Let the world go on fretting about Laura and Petrarch if it will; but as for me, my tears and my lamentations shall be lavished upon the unsung defendant.

We saw also an autograph letter of Lucrezia Borgia, a lady for whom I have always entertained the highest respect, on account of her rare histrionic capabilities, her opulence in solid gold goblets made of gilded wood, her high distinction as an operatic screamer, and the facility with which she could order a sextuple funeral and get the corpses ready for it. We saw one single coarse yellow hair from Lucrezia's head, likewise. It awoke emotions, but we still live. In this same library we saw some drawings by Michael Angelo (these Italians call him Mickel Angelo) and Leonardo da Vinci. (They spell it Vinci and pronounce it Vinchy; foreigners always spell better than they pronounce.) We reserve our opinion of these sketches.

In another building they showed us a fresco representing some lions and other beasts drawing chariots; and they seemed to project so far from the wall that we took them to be sculptures. The artist had shrewdly heightened the delusion by painting dust on the creatures' backs, as if it had fallen there naturally and properly. Smart fellow – if it be smart to deceive strangers.

Elsewhere we saw a huge Roman amphitheater, with its stone seats still in good preservation. Modernized, it is now the scene of more peaceful recreations than the exhibition of a party of wild beasts with Christians for dinner. Part of the time, the Milanese use it for a race track, and at other seasons they flood it with water and have spirited yachting regattas there. The guide told us these things, and he would hardly try so hazardous an experiment as the telling of a falsehood, when it is all he can do to speak the truth in English without getting the lock-jaw.

In another place we were shown a sort of summer arbor, with a fence before it. We said that was nothing. We looked again, and saw, through the arbor, an endless stretch of garden, and shrubbery, and grassy lawn. We were perfectly willing to go in there and rest, but it could not be done. It was only another delusion – a painting by some ingenious artist with little charity in his heart for tired folk. The deception was perfect. No one could have imagined the park was not real. We even thought we smelled the flowers at first.

We got a carriage at twilight and drove in the shaded avenues with the other nobility, and after dinner we took wine and ices in a fine garden with the great public. The music was excellent, the flowers and shrubbery were pleasant to the eye, the scene was vivacious, everybody was genteel and well-behaved, and the ladies were slightly moustached, and handsomely dressed, but very homely.

We adjourned to a cafe and played billiards an hour, and I made six or seven points by the doctor pocketing his ball, and he made as many by my pocketing my ball. We came near making a carom sometimes, but not the one we were trying to make. The table was of the usual European style – cushions dead and twice as high as the balls; the cues in bad repair. The natives play only a sort of pool on them. We have never seen anybody playing the French three-ball game yet, and I doubt if there is any such game known in France, or that there lives any man mad enough to try to play it on one of these European tables. We had to stop playing finally because Dan got to sleeping fifteen minutes between the counts and paying no attention to his marking.

Afterward we walked up and down one of the most popular streets for some time, enjoying other people's comfort and wishing we could export some of it to our restless, driving, vitality-consuming marts at home. Just in this one matter lies the main charm of life in Europe – comfort. In America, we hurry – which is well; but when the day's work is done, we go on thinking of losses and gains, we plan for the morrow, we even carry our business cares to bed with us, and toss and worry over them when we ought to be restoring our racked bodies and brains with sleep. We burn up our energies with these excitements, and either die early or drop into a lean and mean old age at a time of life which they call a man's prime in Europe. When an acre of ground has produced long and well, we let it lie fallow and rest for a season; we take no man clear across the continent in the same coach he started in – the coach is stabled somewhere on the plains and its heated machinery allowed to cool for a few days; when a razor has seen long service and refuses to hold an edge, the barber lays it away for a few weeks, and the edge comes back of its own accord. We bestow thoughtful care upon inanimate objects, but none upon ourselves. What a robust people, what a nation of thinkers we might be, if we would only lay ourselves on the shelf occasionally and renew our edges!

I do envy these Europeans the comfort they take. When the work of the day is done, they forget it. Some of them go, with wife and children, to a beer hall and sit quietly and genteelly drinking a mug or two of ale and listening to music; others walk the streets, others drive in the avenues; others assemble in the great ornamental squares in the early evening to enjoy the sight and the fragrance of flowers and to hear the military bands play – no European city being without its fine military music at eventide; and yet others of the populace sit in the open air in front of the refreshment houses and eat ices and drink mild beverages that could not harm a child. They go to bed moderately early, and sleep well. They are always quiet, always orderly, always cheerful, comfortable, and appreciative of life and its manifold blessings. One never sees a drunken man among them. The change that has come over our little party is surprising. Day by day we lose some of our restlessness and absorb some of the spirit of quietude and ease that is in the tranquil atmosphere about us and in the demeanor of the people. We grow wise apace. We begin to comprehend what life is for.

We have had a bath in Milan, in a public bath-house. They were going to put all three of us in one bath-tub, but we objected. Each of us had an Italian farm on his back. We could have felt affluent if we had been officially surveyed and fenced in. We chose to have three bathtubs, and large ones – tubs suited to the dignity of aristocrats who had real estate, and brought it with them. After we were stripped and had taken the first chilly dash, we discovered that haunting atrocity that has embittered our lives in so many cities and villages of Italy and France – there was no soap. I called. A woman answered, and I barely had time to throw myself against the door – she would have been in, in another second. I said:

'Beware, woman! Go away from here – go away, now, or it will be the worse for you. I am an unprotected male, but I will preserve my honor at the peril of my life!'

These words must have frightened her, for she scurried away very fast.

Dan's voice rose on the air:

'Oh, bring some soap, why don't you!'

The reply was Italian. Dan resumed:

'Soap, you know – soap. That is what I want – soap. S-o-a-p, soap; s-o-p-e, soap; s-o-u-p, soap. Hurry up! I don't know how you Irish spell it, but I want it. Spell it to suit yourself, but fetch it. I'm freezing.'

I heard the doctor say impressively:

'Dan, how often have we told you that these foreigners cannot understand English? Why will you not depend upon us? Why will you not tell *us* what you want, and let us ask for it in the language of the country? It would save us a great deal of the humiliation your reprehensible ignorance causes us. I will address this person in his mother tongue: "Here, cospetto! corpo di Bacco! Sacramento! Solferino! – Soap, you son of a gun!" Dan, if you would let *us* talk for you, you would never expose your ignorant vulgarity.'

Even this fluent discharge of Italian did not bring the soap at once, but there was a good reason for it. There was not such an article about the establishment. It is my belief that there never had been. They had to send far up town, and to several different places before they finally got it, so they said. We had to wait twenty or thirty minutes. The same thing had occurred the evening before, at the hotel. I think I have divined the reason for this state of things at last. The English know how to travel comfortably, and they carry soap with them; other foreigners do not use the article.

At every hotel we stop at we always have to send out for soap, at the last moment, when we are grooming ourselves for dinner, and they put it in the bill along with the candles and other nonsense. In Marseilles they make half the fancy toilet soap we consume in

America, but the Marseillais only have a vague theoretical idea of its use, which they have obtained from books of travel, just as they have acquired an uncertain notion of clean shirts, and the peculiarities of the gorilla, and other curious matters. This reminds me of poor Blucher's note to the landlord in Paris:

> PARIS, LE 7 JUILLET.
> *Monsieur le Landlord* – Sir: *Pourquoi* don't you *mettez* some *savon* in your bedchambers? *Est-ce que vous pensez* I will steal it? *La nuit passée* you charged me *pour deux chandelles* when I only had one; *hier vous avez* charged me *avec glace* when I had none at all; *tout les jours* you are coming some fresh game or other on me, *mais vous ne pouvez pas* play this *savon* dodge on me twice. *Savon* is a necessary *de la vie* to anybody but a Frenchman, et *je l'aurai hors de cet hotel* or make trouble. You hear *me. Allons.*
> BLUCHER.

I remonstrated against the sending of this note, because it was so mixed up that the landlord would never be able to make head or tail of it; but Blucher said he guessed the old man could read the French of it and average the rest.

Blucher's French is bad enough, but it is not much worse than the English one finds in advertisements all over Italy every day. For instance, observe the printed card of the hotel we shall probably stop at on the shores of Lake Como:

NOTISH.

This hotel which best it is in Italy and most superb, is handsome locate on the best situation of the lake, with the most splendid view near the Villas Melzy, to the King of Belgian, and Serbelloni. This hotel have recently enlarge, do offer all commodities on moderate price, at the strangers gentlemen who whish spend the seasons on the Lake Come.

How is that, for a specimen? In the hotel is a handsome little chapel where an English clergyman is employed to preach to such of the guests of the house as hail from England and America, and this fact is also set forth in barbarous English in the same advertisement. Wouldn't you have supposed that the adventurous linguist who framed the card would have known enough to submit it to that clergyman before he sent it to the printer?

Here in Milan, in an ancient tumble-down ruin of a church, is the mournful wreck of the most celebrated painting in the world – 'The Last Supper', by Leonardo da Vinci. We are not infallible judges of pictures, but of course we went there to see this wonderful painting, once so beautiful, always so worshipped by masters in art, and forever to be famous in song and story. And the first thing that occurred was the infliction on us of a placard fairly reeking with wretched English. Take a morsel of it:

> Bartholomew (that is the first figure on the left hand side at the spectator,) uncertain and doubtful about what he thinks to have heard, and upon which he wants to be assured by himself at Christ and by no others.

Good, isn't it? And then Peter is described as 'argumenting in a threatening and angrily condition at Judas Iscariot'.

This paragraph recalls the picture. 'The Last Supper' is painted on the dilapidated wall of what was a little chapel attached to the main church in ancient times, I suppose. It is battered and scarred in every direction, and stained and discolored by time, and Napoleon's horses kicked the legs off most the disciples when they (the horses, not the disciples,) were stabled there more than half a century ago.

I recognized the old picture in a moment – the Saviour with bowed head seated at the center of a long, rough table with scattering fruits and dishes upon it, and six disciples on either side in their long robes, talking to each other – the picture from which all engravings and all copies have been made for three centuries. Perhaps no living man has ever known an attempt to paint the

Lord's Supper differently. The world seems to have become settled in the belief, long ago, that it is not possible for human genius to outdo this creation of da Vinci's. I suppose painters will go on copying it as long as any of the original is left visible to the eye. There were a dozen easels in the room, and as many artists transferring the great picture to their canvases. Fifty proofs of steel engravings and lithographs were scattered around, too. And as usual, I could not help noticing how superior the copies were to the original, that is, to my inexperienced eye. Wherever you find a Raphael, a Rubens, a Michelangelo, a Carracci, or a da Vinci (and we see them every day,) you find artists copying them, and the copies are always the handsomest. Maybe the originals were handsome when they were new, but they are not now.

The colors are dimmed with age; the countenances are scaled and marred, and nearly all expression is gone from them; the hair is a dead blur upon the wall, and there is no life in the eyes. Only the attitudes are certain.

People come here from all parts of the world, and glorify this masterpiece. They stand entranced before it with bated breath and parted lips, and when they speak, it is only in the catchy ejaculations of rapture:

'Oh, wonderful!'

'Such expression!'

'Such grace of attitude!'

'Such dignity!'

'Such faultless drawing!'

'Such matchless coloring!'

'Such feeling!'

'What delicacy of touch!'

'What sublimity of conception!'

'A vision! A vision!'

I only envy these people; I envy them their honest admiration, if it be honest – their delight, if they feel delight. I harbor no animosity toward any of them. But at the same time the thought *will* intrude itself upon me, How can they see what is not visible? What would you think of a man who looked at some decayed, blind, toothless, pock-marked Cleopatra, and said: 'What matchless beauty! What soul! What expression!' What would you think of a man who gazed upon a dingy, foggy sunset, and said: 'What sublimity! What feeling! What richness of coloring!' What would you think of a man who stared in ecstasy upon a desert of stumps and said: 'Oh, my soul, my beating heart, what a noble forest is here!'

You would think that those men had an astonishing talent for seeing things that had already passed away. It was what I thought when I stood before 'The Last Supper' and heard men apostrophizing wonders, and beauties and perfections which had faded out of the picture and gone, a hundred years before they were born. We can imagine the beauty that was once in an aged face; we can imagine the forest if we *see* the stumps; but we cannot absolutely see these things when they are not there. I am willing to believe that the eye of the practiced artist can rest upon the Last Supper and renew a lustre where only a hint of it is left, supply a tint that has faded away, restore an expression that is gone; patch, and color, and add, to the dull canvas until at last its figures shall stand before him aglow with the life, the feeling, the freshness, yea, with all the noble beauty that was theirs when first they came from the hand of the master. But I cannot work this miracle. Can those other uninspired visitors do it, or do they only happily imagine they do?

After reading so much about it, I am satisfied that the Last Supper was a very miracle of art once. But it was 300 years ago.

It vexes me to hear people talk so glibly of 'feeling', 'expression', 'tone' and those other easily acquired and inexpensive technicalities of art that make such a fine show in conversations concerning pictures. There is not one man in 7,500 that can tell *what* a pictured face is intended to express. There is not one man in 500 that can go into a courtroom and be sure that he will not mistake some harmless innocent of a juryman for the black-hearted assassin on trial. Yet such people talk of 'character' and presume to interpret 'expression' in pictures. There is an old story that Matthews, the actor, was once lauding the ability of the human face to express the passions and emotions hidden in the breast. He said the countenance could disclose what was passing in the heart plainer than the tongue could.

'Now,' he said, 'observe my face – what does it express?'

'Despair!'

'Bah, it expresses peaceful resignation! What does this express?'

'Rage!'

'Stuff! It means terror! *This*!'

'Imbecility!'

'Fool! It is smothered ferocity! Now *this*!'

'Joy!'

'Oh, perdition! *Any ass* can see it means insanity!'

Expression! People coolly pretend to read it who would think themselves presumptuous if they pretended to interpret the hieroglyphics on the obelisks of Luxor – yet they are fully as competent to do the one thing as the other. I have heard two very intelligent critics speak of Murillo's 'Immaculate Conception' (now in the museum at Seville,) within the past few days. One said:

'Oh, the Virgin's face is full of the ecstasy of a joy that is complete – that leaves nothing more to be desired on earth!'

The other said:

'Ah, that wonderful face is so humble, so pleading – it says as plainly as words could say it: "I fear; I tremble; I am unworthy. But Thy will be done; sustain Thou Thy servant!"'

The reader can see the picture in any drawing room; it can be easily recognized: the Virgin (the only young and really beautiful Virgin that was ever painted by one of the old masters, some of us think,) stands in the crescent of the new moon, with a multitude of cherubs hovering about her, and more coming; her hands are crossed upon her breast, and upon her uplifted countenance falls a glory out of the heavens. The reader may amuse himself, if he chooses, in trying to determine which of these gentlemen read the Virgin's 'expression' aright, or if either of them did it.

Anyone who is acquainted with the old masters will comprehend how much 'The Last Supper' is damaged when I say that the spectator cannot really tell, now, whether the disciples are Hebrews or Italians. These ancient painters never succeeded in denationalizing themselves. The Italian artists painted Italian Virgins, the Dutch painted Dutch Virgins, the Virgins of the French painters were Frenchwomen – none of them ever put into the face of the Madonna that indescribable something which proclaims the Jewess, whether you find her in New York, in Constantinople, in Paris, Jerusalem, or in the empire of Morocco. I saw in the Sandwich Islands, once, a picture copied by a talented German artist from an engraving in one of the American illustrated papers. It was an allegory, representing Mr Davis in the act of signing a secession act or some such document. Over him hovered the ghost of Washington in warning attitude, and in the background a troop of shadowy soldiers in Continental uniform were limping with shoeless, bandaged feet through a driving snow-storm. Valley Forge was suggested, of course. The copy seemed accurate, and yet there was a discrepancy somewhere. After a long examination I discovered what it was – the shadowy soldiers were all Germans! Jeff Davis was a German! even the hovering ghost was a German ghost! The artist had unconsciously worked his nationality into the picture. To tell the truth, I am getting a little perplexed about John the Baptist and his portraits. In France I finally grew reconciled to him as a Frenchman; here he is unquestionably an Italian. What next? Can it be possible that the painters make John the Baptist a Spaniard in Madrid and an Irishman in Dublin?

We left Milan by rail. The Cathedral six or seven miles behind us; vast, dreamy, bluish, snow-clad mountains twenty miles in front of us, – these were the accented points in the scenery. The more immediate scenery consisted of fields and farmhouses outside the car and a monster-headed dwarf and a moustached woman inside it. These latter were not show-people. Alas, deformity and female beards are too common in Italy to attract attention.

We passed through a range of wild, picturesque hills, steep, wooded, cone-shaped, with rugged crags projecting here and there, and with dwellings and ruinous castles perched away up toward the drifting clouds. We lunched at the curious old town of Como, at the foot of the lake, and then took the small steamer and had an afternoon's pleasure excursion to this place, – Bellaggio.

When we walked ashore, a party of policemen (people whose cocked hats and showy uniforms would shame the finest uniform in the military service of the United States,) put us into a little stone cell and locked us in. We had the whole passenger list for company, but their room would have been preferable, for there was no light, there were no windows, no ventilation. It was close and hot. We were much crowded. It was the Black Hole of Calcutta on a small scale. Presently a smoke rose about our feet – a smoke that smelled of all the dead things of earth, of all the putrefaction and corruption imaginable.

We were there five minutes, and when we got out it was hard to tell which of us carried the vilest fragrance.

These miserable outcasts called that 'fumigating' us, and the term was a tame one indeed. They fumigated us to guard themselves against the cholera, though we hailed from no infected port. We had left the cholera far behind us all the time. However, they must keep epidemics away somehow or other, and fumigation is cheaper than soap. They must either wash themselves or fumigate other people. Some of the lower classes had rather die than wash, but the fumigation of strangers causes them no pangs. They need no fumigation themselves. Their habits make it unnecessary. They carry their preventive with them; they sweat and fumigate all day long. I trust I am a humble and a consistent Christian. I try to do what is right. I know it is my duty to 'pray for them that despitefully use me'; and therefore, hard as it is, I shall still try to pray for these fumigating, macaroni-stuffing organ-grinders.

Our hotel sits at the water's edge – at least its front garden does – and we walk among the shrubbery and smoke at twilight; we look afar off at Switzerland and the Alps, and feel an indolent willingness to look no closer; we go down the steps and swim in the lake; we take a shapely little boat and sail abroad among the reflections of the stars; lie on the thwarts and listen to the distant laughter, the singing, the soft melody of flutes and guitars that comes floating across the water from pleasuring gondolas; we close the evening with exasperating billiards on one of those same old execrable tables. A midnight luncheon in our ample bedchamber; a final smoke in its contracted veranda facing the water, the gardens, and the mountains; a summing up of the day's events. Then to bed, with drowsy brains harassed with a mad panorama that mixes up pictures of France, of Italy, of the ship, of the ocean, of home, in grotesque and bewildering disorder. Then a melting away of familiar faces, of cities, and of tossing waves, into a great calm of forgetfulness and peace.

After which, the nightmare.

Breakfast in the morning, and then the lake.

I did not like it yesterday. I thought Lake Tahoe was *much* finer. I have to confess now, however, that my judgment erred somewhat, though not extravagantly. I always had an idea that Como was a vast basin of water, like Tahoe, shut in by great mountains. Well, the border of huge mountains is here, but the lake itself is not a basin. It is as crooked as any brook, and only from one-quarter to two-thirds as wide as the Mississippi. There is not a yard of low ground on either side of it – nothing but endless chains of mountains that spring abruptly from the water's edge and tower to altitudes varying from a thousand to two thousand feet. Their craggy sides are clothed with vegetation, and white specks of houses peep out from the luxuriant foliage everywhere; they are even perched upon jutting and picturesque pinnacles a thousand feet above your head.

Again, for miles along the shores, handsome country seats, surrounded by gardens and groves, sit fairly in the water, sometimes in nooks carved by Nature out of the vine-hung precipices, and with no ingress or egress save by boats. Some have great broad stone staircases leading down to the water, with heavy stone balustrades ornamented with statuary and fancifully adorned with creeping vines and bright-colored flowers – for all the world like a drop curtain in a theater, and lacking nothing but long-waisted, high-heeled women and plumed gallants in silken tights coming down to go serenading in the splendid gondola in waiting.

A great feature of Como's attractiveness is the multitude of pretty houses and gardens that cluster upon its shores and on its mountain sides. They look so snug and so homelike, and at eventide when everything seems to slumber, and the music of the vesper bells comes stealing over the water, one almost believes that nowhere else than on the lake of Como can there be found such a paradise of tranquil repose.

From my window here in Bellaggio, I have a view of the other side of the lake now, which is as beautiful as a picture. A scarred and wrinkled precipice rises to a height of 1,800 feet; on a tiny bench half way up its vast wall, sits a little snowflake of a church, no bigger than a martin-box, apparently; skirting the base of the cliff are a hundred orange groves and gardens, flecked with glimpses of the white dwellings that are buried in them; in front, three or four gondolas lie idle upon the water – and in the burnished mirror of the lake, mountain, chapel, houses, groves and boats are counterfeited so brightly and so clearly that one scarce knows where the reality leaves off and the reflection begins!

The surroundings of this picture are fine. A mile away, a grove-plumed promontory juts far into the lake and glasses its palace in the blue depths; in midstream a boat is cutting the shining surface and leaving a long track behind, like a ray of light; the mountains beyond are veiled in a dreamy purple haze; far in the opposite direction a tumbled mass of domes and verdant slopes and valleys bars the lake, and here indeed does distance lend enchantment to the view – for on this broad canvas, sun and clouds and the richest of atmospheres have blended a thousand tints together, and over its surface the filmy lights and shadows drift, hour after hour, and glorify it with a beauty that seems reflected out of Heaven itself. Beyond all question, this is the most voluptuous scene we have yet looked upon.

Last night the scenery was striking and picturesque. On the other side crags and trees and snowy houses were reflected in the lake with a wonderful distinctness, and streams of light from many a distant window shot far abroad over the still waters. On this side, near at hand, great mansions, white with moonlight, glared out from the midst of masses of foliage that lay black and shapeless in the shadows that fell from the cliff above – and down in the margin of the lake every feature of the weird vision was faithfully repeated.

Today we have idled through a wonder of a garden attached to a ducal estate – but enough of description is enough, I judge.

I suspect that this was the same place the gardener's son deceived the Lady of Lyons with, but I do not know. You may have heard of the passage somewhere:

> *A deep vale,*
> *Shut out by Alpine hills from the rude world,*
> *Near a clear lake margined by fruits of gold*
> *And whispering myrtles:*
> *Glassing softest skies, cloudless,*
> *Save with rare and roseate shadows;*
> *A palace, lifting to eternal heaven its marbled walls,*
> *From out a glossy bower of coolest foliage musical with birds.*

That is all very well, except the 'clear' part of the lake. It certainly is clearer than a great many lakes, but how dull its waters are compared with the wonderful transparence of Lake Tahoe! I speak of the north shore of Tahoe, where one can count the scales on a trout at a depth of 180 feet. I have tried to get this statement off at par here, but with no success; so I have been obliged to negotiate it at fifty percent discount. At this rate I find some takers; perhaps the reader will receive it on the same terms – 90 feet instead of 180. But let it be remembered that those are forced terms – Sheriff's sale prices. As far as I am privately concerned, I abate not a jot of the original assertion that in those strangely magnifying waters one may count the scales on a trout (a trout of the large kind,) at a depth of 180 feet – may see every pebble on the bottom – might even count a paper of dray-pins. People talk of the transparent waters of the Mexican Bay of Acapulco, but in my own experience I know they cannot compare with those I am speaking of. I have fished for trout, in Tahoe, and at a measured depth of 84 feet I have seen them put their noses to the bait and I could see their gills open and shut. I could hardly have seen the trout themselves at that distance in the open air.

As I go back in spirit and recall that noble sea, reposing among the snow-peaks 6,000 feet above the ocean, the conviction comes strong upon me again that Como would only seem a bedizened little courtier in that august presence.

Sorrow and misfortune overtake the legislature that still from year to year permits Tahoe to retain its unmusical cognomen! Tahoe! It suggests no crystal waters, no picturesque shores, no sublimity. Tahoe for a sea in the clouds: a sea that has character and asserts it in solemn calms at times, at times in savage storms; a sea whose royal seclusion is guarded by a cordon of sentinel peaks that lift their frosty fronts 9,000 feet above the level world; a sea whose every aspect is impressive, whose belongings are all beautiful, whose lonely majesty types the Deity!

Tahoe means grasshoppers. It means grasshopper soup. It is Indian, and suggestive of Indians. They say it is Piute – possibly it is Digger. I am satisfied it was named by the Diggers – those degraded savages who roast their dead relatives, then mix the human grease and ashes of bones with tar, and 'gaum' it thick all over their heads and foreheads and ears, and go caterwauling about the hills and call it *mourning*. *These* are the gentry that named the Lake.

People say that Tahoe means 'Silver Lake' – 'Limpid Water' – 'Falling Leaf'. Bosh. It means grasshopper soup, the favorite dish of the Digger tribe, – and of the Piutes as well. It isn't worthwhile, in these practical times, for people to talk about Indian poetry – there never was any in them – except in the Fenimore Cooper Indians. But *they* are an extinct tribe that never existed. I know the Noble Red Man. I have camped with the Indians; I have been on the warpath with them, taken part in the chase with them – for grasshoppers; helped them steal cattle; I have roamed with them, scalped them, had them for breakfast. I would gladly eat the whole race if I had a chance.

But I am growing unreliable. I will return to my comparison of the lakes. Como is a little deeper than Tahoe, if people here tell the truth. They say it is 1,800 feet deep at this point, but it does not look a dead enough blue for that. Tahoe is 1,525 feet deep in the center, by the state geologist's measurement. They say the great peak opposite this town is 5,000 feet high: but I feel sure that 3,000 feet of that statement is a good honest lie. The lake is a mile wide, here, and maintains about that width from this point to its northern extremity – which is distant 16 miles: from here to its southern extremity – say 15 miles – it is not over half a mile wide in any place, I should think. Its snow-clad mountains one hears so much about are only seen occasionally, and then in the distance, the Alps. Tahoe is from 10 to 18 miles wide, and its mountains shut it in like a wall. Their summits are never free from snow the year round. One thing about it is very strange: it never has even a skim of ice upon its surface, although lakes in the same range of mountains, lying in a lower and warmer temperature, freeze over in winter.

❧

This Venice, which was a haughty, invincible, magnificent Republic for nearly 1,400 years; whose armies compelled the world's applause whenever and wherever they battled; whose navies well nigh held dominion of the seas, and whose merchant fleets whitened the remotest oceans with their sails and loaded these piers with the products of every clime, is fallen a prey to poverty, neglect and melancholy decay. Six hundred years ago, Venice was the Autocrat of Commerce; her mart was the great commercial center, the distributing-house from whence the enormous trade of the Orient was spread abroad over the Western world. Today her piers are deserted, her warehouses are empty, her merchant fleets are vanished, her armies and her navies are but memories. Her glory is departed, and with her crumbling grandeur of wharves and palaces about her she sits among her stagnant lagoons, forlorn and beggared, forgotten of the world. She that in her palmy days commanded the commerce of a hemisphere and made the weal or woe of nations with a beck of her puissant finger, is become the humblest among the peoples of the earth, – a peddler of glass beads for women, and trifling toys and trinkets for school-girls and children.

The venerable Mother of the Republics is scarce a fit subject for flippant speech or the idle gossipping of tourists. It seems a sort of sacrilege to disturb the glamour of old romance that pictures her to us softly from afar off as through a tinted mist, and curtains her ruin and her desolation from our view. One ought, indeed, to turn away from her rags, her poverty and her humiliation, and think of her only as she was when she sunk the fleets of Charlemagne; when she humbled Frederick Barbarossa or waved her victorious banners above the battlements of Constantinople.

We reached Venice at eight in the evening, and entered a hearse belonging to the Grand Hotel d'Europe. At any rate, it was more like a hearse than anything else, though to speak by the card, it was a gondola. And this was the storied gondola of Venice! – the fairy boat in which the princely cavaliers of the olden time were wont to cleave the waters of the moonlit canals and look the eloquence of love into the soft eyes of patrician beauties, while the gay gondolier in silken doublet touched his guitar and sang as only gondoliers can sing! This the famed gondola and this the gorgeous gondolier! – the one an inky, rusty old canoe with a sable hearse-body clapped on to the middle of it, and the other a mangy, barefooted guttersnipe with a portion of his raiment on exhibition which should have been sacred from public scrutiny. Presently, as he turned a corner and shot his hearse into a dismal ditch between two long rows of towering, untenanted buildings, the gay gondolier began to sing, true to the traditions of his race. I stood it a little while. Then I said:

'Now, here, Roderigo Gonzales Michael Angelo, I'm a pilgrim, and I'm a stranger, but I am not going to have my feelings lacerated by any such caterwauling as that. If that goes on, one of us has got to take water. It is enough that my cherished dreams of Venice have been blighted forever as to the romantic gondola and the gorgeous gondolier; this system of destruction shall go no farther; I will accept the hearse, under protest, and you may fly your flag of truce in peace, but here I register a dark and bloody oath that you shan't sing. Another yelp, and overboard you go.'

I began to feel that the old Venice of song and story had departed forever. But I was too hasty. In a few minutes we swept gracefully out into the Grand Canal, and under the mellow moonlight the Venice of poetry and romance stood revealed. Right from the water's edge rose long lines of stately palaces of marble; gondolas were gliding swiftly hither and thither and disappearing suddenly through unsuspected gates and alleys; ponderous stone bridges threw their shadows athwart the glittering waves. There was life and motion everywhere, and yet everywhere there was a hush, a stealthy sort of stillness, that was suggestive of secret enterprises of bravoes and of lovers; and clad half in moonbeams and half in mysterious shadows, the grim old mansions of the Republic seemed to have an expression about them of having an eye out for just such enterprises as these at that same moment. Music came floating over the waters – Venice was complete.

It was a beautiful picture – very soft and dreamy and beautiful. But what was this Venice to compare with the Venice of midnight? Nothing. There was a fete – a grand fete in honor of some saint who had been instrumental in checking the cholera 300 years ago, and all Venice was abroad on the water. It was no common affair, for the Venetians did not know how soon they might need the saint's services again, now that the cholera was spreading everywhere. So in one vast space – say a third of a mile wide and two miles long – were collected 2,000 gondolas, and every one of them had from two to ten, twenty and even thirty colored lanterns suspended about it, and from four to a dozen occupants. Just as far as the eye could reach, these painted lights were massed together – like a vast garden of many-colored flowers, except that these blossoms were never still; they were ceaselessly gliding in and out, and mingling together, and seducing you into bewildering attempts to follow their mazy evolutions. Here and there a strong red, green, or blue glare from a rocket that was struggling to get away, splendidly illuminated all the boats around it. Every gondola that swam by us, with its crescents and pyramids and circles of colored lamps hung aloft, and lighting up the faces of the young and the sweet-scented and lovely below, was a picture; and the reflections of those lights, so long, so slender, so numberless, so many-colored and so distorted and wrinkled by the waves, was a picture likewise, and one that was enchantingly beautiful. Many and many a party of young ladies and gentlemen had their state gondolas handsomely decorated, and ate supper on board, bringing their swallow-tailed, white-cravatted varlets to wait upon them, and having their tables tricked out as if for a bridal supper. They had brought along the costly globe lamps from their drawing-rooms, and the lace and silken curtains from the same places, I suppose. And they had also brought pianos and guitars, and they played and sang operas, while the plebeian paper-lanterned gondolas from the suburbs and the back alleys crowded around to stare and listen.

There was music everywhere – choruses, string bands, brass bands, flutes, everything. I was so surrounded, walled in, with music, magnificence and loveliness, that I became inspired with the spirit of the scene, and sang one tune myself. However, when I observed that the other gondolas had sailed away, and my gondolier was preparing to go overboard, I stopped.

The fete was magnificent. They kept it up the whole night long, and I never enjoyed myself better than I did while it lasted.

What a funny old city this Queen of the Adriatic is! Narrow streets, vast, gloomy marble palaces, black with the corroding damps of centuries, and all partly submerged; no dry land visible anywhere, and no sidewalks worth mentioning; if you want to go to church, to the theater, or to the restaurant, you must call a gondola. It must be a paradise for cripples, for verily a man has no use for legs here.

For a day or two the place looked so like an overflowed Arkansas town, because of its currentless waters laving the very doorsteps of all the houses, and the cluster of boats made fast under the windows, or skimming in and out of the alleys and byways, that I could not get rid of the impression that there was nothing the matter here but a spring freshet, and that the river would fall in a few weeks and leave a dirty high-water mark on the houses, and the streets full of mud and rubbish.

In the glare of day, there is little poetry about Venice, but under the charitable moon her stained palaces are white again, their battered sculptures are hidden in shadows, and the old city seems crowned once more with the grandeur that was hers 500 years ago. It is easy, then, in fancy, to people these silent canals with plumed gallants and fair ladies – with Shylocks in gaberdine and sandals, venturing loans upon the rich argosies of Venetian commerce – with Othellos and Desdemonas, with Iagos and Roderigos – with noble fleets and victorious legions returning from the wars. In the treacherous sunlight we see Venice decayed, forlorn, poverty-stricken, and commerceless – forgotten and utterly insignificant. But in the moonlight, her fourteen centuries of greatness fling their glories about her, and once more is she the princeliest among the nations of the earth.

> *There is a glorious city in the sea;*
> *The sea is in the broad, the narrow streets,*
> *Ebbing and flowing; and the salt-sea weed*
> *Clings to the marble of her palaces.*
> *No track of men, no footsteps to and fro,*
> *Lead to her gates! The path lies o'er the sea,*
> *Invisible: and from the land we went,*
> *As to a floating city – steering in,*
> *And gliding up her streets, as in a dream,*
> *So smoothly, silently – by many a dome,*
> *Mosque-like, and many a stately portico,*
> *The statues ranged along an azure sky;*
> *By many a pile, in more than Eastern pride,*

Of old the residence of merchant kings;
The fronts of some, tho' time had shatter'd them,
Still glowing with the richest hues of art,
As tho' the wealth within them had run o'er.

What would one naturally wish to see first in Venice? The Bridge of Sighs, of course – and next the Church and the Great Square of St Mark, the Bronze Horses, and the famous Lion of St Mark.

We intended to go to the Bridge of Sighs, but happened into the Ducal Palace first – a building which necessarily figures largely in Venetian poetry and tradition. In the Senate Chamber of the ancient Republic we wearied our eyes with staring at acres of historical paintings by Tintoretto and Paul Veronese, but nothing struck us forcibly except the one thing that strikes all strangers forcibly – a black square in the midst of a gallery of portraits. In one long row, around the great hall, were painted the portraits of the Doges of Venice (venerable fellows, with flowing white beards, for of the 300 Senators eligible to the office, the oldest was usually chosen Doge,) and each had its complimentary inscription attached – till you came to the place that should have had Marino Faliero's picture in it, and that was blank and black – blank, except that it bore a terse inscription, saying that the conspirator had died for his crime. It seemed cruel to keep that pitiless inscription still staring from the walls after the unhappy wretch had been in his grave 500 years.

At the head of the Giant's Staircase, where Marino Faliero was beheaded, and where the Doges were crowned in ancient times, two small slits in the stone wall were pointed out – two harmless, insignificant orifices that would never attract a stranger's attention – yet these were the terrible Lions' Mouths! The heads were gone (knocked off by the French during their occupation of Venice) but these were the throats, down which went the anonymous accusation, thrust in secretly at dead of night by an enemy, that doomed many an innocent man to walk the Bridge of Sighs and descend into the dungeon which none entered and hoped to see the sun again. This was in the old days when the Patricians alone governed Venice – the common herd had no vote and no voice. There were 1,500 Patricians; from these, 300 Senators were chosen; from the Senators a Doge and a Council of Ten were selected, and by secret ballot the Ten chose from their own number a Council of Three. All these were Government spies, then, and every spy was under surveillance himself – men spoke in whispers in Venice, and no man trusted his neighbor – not always his own brother. No man knew who the Council of Three were – not even the Senate, not even the Doge; the members of that dread tribunal met at night in a chamber to themselves, masked, and robed from head to foot in scarlet cloaks, and did not even know each other, unless by voice. It was their duty to judge heinous political crimes, and from their sentence there was no appeal. A nod to the executioner was sufficient. The doomed man was marched down a hall and out at a doorway into the covered Bridge of Sighs, through it and into the dungeon and unto his death. At no time in his transit was he visible to any save his conductor. If a man had an enemy in those old days, the cleverest thing he could do was to slip a note for the Council of Three into the Lion's mouth, saying 'This man is plotting against the Government.' If the awful Three found no proof, ten to one they would drown him anyhow, because he was a deep rascal, since his plots were unsolvable. Masked judges and masked executioners, with unlimited power, and no appeal from their judgements, in that hard, cruel age, were not likely to be lenient with men they suspected yet could not convict.

We walked through the hall of the Council of Ten, and presently entered the infernal den of the Council of Three.

The table around which they had sat was there still, and likewise the stations where the masked inquisitors and executioners formerly stood, frozen, upright and silent, till they received a bloody order, and then, without a word, moved off like the inexorable machines they were, to carry it out. The frescoes on the walls were startlingly suited to the place. In all the other saloons, the halls, the great state chambers of the palace, the walls and ceilings were bright with gilding, rich with elaborate carving, and resplendent with gallant pictures of Venetian victories in war, and Venetian display in foreign courts, and hallowed with portraits of the Virgin, the Saviour of men, and the holy saints that preached the Gospel of Peace upon earth – but here, in dismal contrast, were none but pictures of death and dreadful suffering! – not a living figure but was writhing in torture, not a dead one but was smeared with blood, gashed with wounds, and distorted with the agonies that had taken away its life!

From the palace to the gloomy prison is but a step – one might almost jump across the narrow canal that intervenes. The ponderous stone Bridge of Sighs crosses it at the second story – a bridge that is a covered tunnel – you cannot be seen when you walk in it. It is partitioned lengthwise, and through one compartment walked such as bore light sentences in ancient times, and through the other marched sadly the wretches whom the Three had doomed to lingering misery and utter oblivion in the dungeons, or to sudden and mysterious death. Down below the level of the water, by the light of smoking torches, we were shown the damp, thick-walled cells where many a proud patrician's life was eaten away by the long-drawn miseries of solitary imprisonment – without light, air, books; naked, unshaven, uncombed, covered with vermin; his useless tongue forgetting its office, with none to speak to; the days and nights of his life no longer marked, but merged into one eternal eventless night; far away from all cheerful sounds, buried in the silence of a tomb; forgotten by his helpless friends, and his fate a dark mystery to them forever; losing his own memory at last, and knowing no more who he was or how he came there; devouring the loaf of bread and drinking the water that were thrust into the cell by unseen hands, and troubling his worn spirit no more with hopes and fears and doubts and longings to be free; ceasing to scratch vain prayers and complainings on walls where none, not even himself, could see them, and resigning himself to hopeless apathy, driveling childishness, lunacy! Many and many a sorrowful story like this these stony walls could tell if they could but speak.

In a little narrow corridor, near by, they showed us where many a prisoner, after lying in the dungeons until he was forgotten by all save his persecutors, was brought by masked executioners and garroted, or sewed up in a sack, passed through a little window to a boat, at dead of night, and taken to some remote spot and drowned.

They used to show to visitors the implements of torture wherewith the Three were wont to worm secrets out of the accused – villainous machines for crushing thumbs; the stocks where a prisoner sat immovable while water fell drop by drop upon his head till the torture was more than humanity could bear; and a devilish contrivance of steel, which inclosed a prisoner's head like a shell, and crushed it slowly by means of a screw. It bore the stains of blood that had trickled through its joints long ago, and on one side it had a projection whereon the torturer rested his elbow comfortably and bent down his ear to catch the moanings of the sufferer perishing within.

Of course we went to see the venerable relic of the ancient glory of Venice, with its pavements worn and broken by the passing feet of a thousand years of plebeians and patricians – The Cathedral of St Mark. It is built entirely of precious marbles, brought from the Orient – nothing in its composition is domestic. Its hoary traditions make it an object of absorbing interest to even the most careless stranger, and thus far it had interest for me; but no further. I could not go into ecstasies over its coarse mosaics, its unlovely Byzantine architecture, or its 500 curious interior columns from as many distant quarries. Everything was worn out – every block of stone was smooth and almost shapeless with the polishing hands and shoulders of loungers who devoutly idled here in bygone centuries and have died and gone to the dev– no, simply died, I mean.

Under the altar repose the ashes of St Mark – and Matthew, Luke and John, too, for all I know. Venice reveres those relics above all things earthly. For 1,400 years St Mark has been her patron saint. Everything about the city seems to be named after him or so named as to refer to him in some way – so named, or some purchase rigged in some way to scrape a sort of hurrahing acquaintance with him. That seems to be the idea. To be on good terms with St Mark, seems to be the very summit of Venetian ambition. They say St Mark had a tame lion, and used to travel with him – and everywhere that St Mark went, the lion was sure to go. It was his protector, his friend, his librarian. And so the Winged Lion of St Mark, with the open Bible under his paw, is a favorite emblem in the grand old city. It casts its shadow from the most ancient pillar in Venice, in the Grand Square of St Mark, upon the throngs of free citizens below, and has so done for many a long century. The winged lion is found everywhere – and doubtless here, where the winged lion is, no harm can come.

St Mark died at Alexandria, in Egypt. He was martyred, I think. However, that has nothing to do with my legend. About the founding of the city of Venice – say 450 years after Christ – (for Venice is much younger than any other Italian city,) a priest dreamed that an angel told him that until the remains of St Mark were brought to Venice, the city could never rise to high distinction among the nations; that the body must be captured, brought to the city, and a magnificent church built over it; and that if ever the Venetians allowed the Saint to be removed from his new resting-place, in that day Venice would perish from off the face of the earth. The priest proclaimed his dream, and forthwith Venice set about procuring the corpse of St Mark. One expedition after another tried and failed, but the project was never abandoned during 400 years. At last it was secured by stratagem, in the year 800 and something. The commander of a Venetian expedition disguised himself, stole the bones, separated them, and packed them in vessels filled with lard. The religion of Mahomet causes its devotees to abhor anything that is in the nature of pork, and so when the Christian was stopped by the officers at the gates of the city, they only glanced once into his precious baskets, then turned up their noses at the unholy lard, and let him go. The bones were buried in the vaults of the grand cathedral, which had been waiting long years to receive them, and thus the safety and the greatness of Venice were secured. And to this day there be those in Venice who believe that if those holy ashes were stolen away, the ancient city would vanish like a dream, and its foundations be buried forever in the unremembering sea.

❧❦❧

The Venetian gondola is as free and graceful, in its gliding movement, as a serpent. It is twenty or thirty feet long, and is narrow and deep, like a canoe; its sharp bow and stern sweep upward from the water like the horns of a crescent with the abruptness of the curve slightly modified.

The bow is ornamented with a steel comb with a battle-axe attachment which threatens to cut passing boats in two occasionally, but never does. The gondola is painted black because in the zenith of Venetian magnificence the gondolas became too gorgeous altogether, and the Senate decreed that all such display must cease, and a solemn, unembellished black be substituted. If the truth were known, it would doubtless appear that rich plebeians grew too prominent in their affectation of patrician show on the Grand Canal, and required a wholesome snubbing. Reverence for the hallowed past and its traditions keeps the dismal fashion in force now that the compulsion exists no longer. So let it remain. It is the color of mourning. Venice mourns. The stern of the boat is decked over and the gondolier stands there. He uses a single oar – a long blade, of course, for he stands nearly erect. A wooden peg, a foot and a half high, with two slight crooks or curves in one side of it and one in the other, projects above the starboard gunwale.

Against that peg the gondolier takes a purchase with his oar, changing it at intervals to the other side of the peg or dropping it into another of the crooks, as the steering of the craft may demand – and how in the world he can back and fill, shoot straight ahead, or flirt suddenly around a corner, and make the oar stay in those insignificant notches, is a problem to me and a never diminishing matter of interest. I am afraid I study the gondolier's marvelous skill more than I do the sculptured palaces we glide among. He cuts a corner so closely, now and then, or misses another gondola by such an imperceptible hair-breadth that I feel myself 'scrooching', as the children say, just as one does when a buggy wheel grazes his elbow. But he makes all his calculations with the nicest precision, and goes darting in and out among a Broadway confusion of busy craft with the easy confidence of the educated hackman. He never makes a mistake.

Sometimes we go flying down the great canals at such a gait that we can get only the merest glimpses into front doors, and again, in obscure alleys in the suburbs, we put on a solemnity suited to the silence, the mildew, the stagnant waters, the clinging weeds, the deserted houses and the general lifelessness of the place, and move to the spirit of grave meditation.

The gondolier is a picturesque rascal for all he wears no satin harness, no plumed bonnet, no silken tights. His attitude is stately; he is lithe and supple; all his movements are full of grace. When his long canoe, and his fine figure, towering from its high perch on the stern, are cut against the evening sky, they make a picture that is very novel and striking to a foreign eye.

We sit in the cushioned carriage-body of a cabin, with the curtains drawn, and smoke, or read, or look out upon the passing boats, the houses, the bridges, the people, and enjoy ourselves much more than we could in a buggy jolting over our cobblestone pavements at home. This is the gentlest, pleasantest locomotion we have ever known.

But it seems queer – ever so queer – to see a boat doing duty as a private carriage. We see business men come to the front door, step into a gondola, instead of a street car, and go off down town to the counting-room.

We see visiting young ladies stand on the stoop, and laugh, and kiss goodbye, and flirt their fans and say 'Come soon – now *do* – you've been just as mean as ever you can be – mother's dying to see you – and we've moved into the new house, O such a love of a place! – so convenient to the post office and the church, and the Young Men's Christian Association; and we do have such fishing, and such carrying on, and *such* swimming-matches in the backyard!

– Oh, you *must* come – no distance at all, and if you go down through by St Mark's and the Bridge of Sighs, and cut through the alley and come up by the church of Santa Maria dei Frari, and into the Grand Canal, there isn't a *bit* of current – now *do* come, Sally Maria – bye-bye!' and then the little humbug trips down the steps, jumps into the gondola, says, under her breath, 'Disagreeable old thing, I hope she *won't*!' goes skimming away, round the corner; and the other girl slams the street door and says, 'Well, *that* infliction's over, anyway, – but I suppose I've got to go and see her – tiresome stuck-up thing!' Human nature appears to be just the same, all over the world. We see the diffident young man, mild of moustache, affluent of hair, indigent of brain, elegant of costume, drive up to *her* father's mansion, tell his hackman to bail out and wait, start fearfully up the steps and meet 'the old gentleman right on the threshold!' – hear him ask what street the new British Bank is in – as if *that* were what he came for – and then bounce into his boat and skurry away with his coward heart in his boots! – see him come sneaking around the corner again, directly, with a crack of the curtain open toward the old gentleman's disappearing gondola, and out scampers his Susan with a flock of little Italian endearments fluttering from her lips, and goes to drive with him in the watery avenues down toward the Rialto.

We see the ladies go out shopping, in the most natural way, and flit from street to street and from store to store, just in the good old fashion, except that they leave the gondola, instead of a private carriage, waiting at the curbstone a couple of hours for them, – waiting while they make the nice young clerks pull down tons and tons of silks and velvets and moire antiques and those things; and then they buy a paper of pins and go paddling away to confer the rest of their disastrous patronage on some other firm. And they always have their purchases sent home just in the good old way. Human nature is very much the same all over the world; and it is so like my dear native home to see a Venetian lady go into a store and buy ten cents' worth of blue ribbon and have it sent home in a scow. Ah, it is these little touches of nature that move one to tears in these far-off foreign lands.

We see little girls and boys go out in gondolas with their nurses, for an airing. We see staid families, with prayer-book and beads, enter the gondola dressed in their Sunday best, and float away to church. And at midnight we see the theater break up and discharge its swarm of hilarious youth and beauty; we hear the cries of the hackman-gondoliers, and behold the struggling crowd jump aboard, and the black multitude of boats go skimming down the moonlit avenues; we see them separate here and there, and disappear up divergent streets; we hear the faint sounds of laughter and of shouted farewells floating up out of the distance; and then, the strange pageant being gone, we have lonely stretches of glittering water – of stately buildings – of blotting shadows – of weird stone faces creeping into the moonlight – of deserted bridges – of motionless boats at anchor. And over all broods that mysterious stillness, that stealthy quiet, that befits so well this old dreaming Venice.

We have been pretty much everywhere in our gondola. We have bought beads and photographs in the stores, and wax matches in the Great Square of St Mark. The last remark suggests a digression. Everybody goes to this vast square in the evening. The military bands play in the center of it and countless couples of ladies and gentlemen promenade up and down on either side, and platoons of them are constantly drifting away toward the old Cathedral, and by the venerable column with the Winged Lion of St Mark on its top, and out to where the boats lie moored; and other platoons are as constantly arriving from the gondolas and joining the great throng. Between the promenaders and the sidewalks are seated hundreds and hundreds of people at small tables, smoking and taking *granita* (a first cousin to ice-cream) on the sidewalks are more employing themselves in the same way. The shops in the first floor of the tall rows of buildings that wall in three sides of the square are brilliantly lighted, the air is filled with music and merry voices, and altogether the scene is as bright and spirited and full of cheerfulness as any man could desire. We enjoy it thoroughly. Very many of the young women are exceedingly pretty and dress with rare good taste. We are gradually and laboriously learning the ill-manners of staring them unflinchingly in the face – not because such conduct is agreeable to us, but because it is the custom of the country and they say the girls like it. We wish to learn all the curious, outlandish ways of all the different countries, so that we can 'show off' and astonish people when we get home. We wish to excite the envy of our untraveled friends with our strange foreign fashions which we can't shake off. All our passengers are paying strict attention to this thing, with the end in view which I have mentioned. The gentle reader will never, never know what a consummate ass he can become, until he goes abroad. I speak now, of course, in the supposition that the gentle reader has not been abroad, and therefore is not already a consummate ass. If the case be otherwise, I beg his pardon and extend to him the cordial hand of fellowship and call him brother. I shall always delight to meet an ass after my own heart when I shall have finished my travels.

On this subject let me remark that there are Americans abroad in Italy who have actually forgotten their mother tongue in three months – forgot it in France. They cannot even write their address in English in a hotel register. I append these evidences, which I copied verbatim from the register of a hotel in a certain Italian city:

John P. Whitcomb, *Etats Unis*.

Wm. L. Ainsworth, *travailleur* [he meant traveler, I suppose], *Etats Unis*.

George P. Morton et fils, d'Amerique.

Lloyd B. Williams, et trois amis, ville de Boston, Amerique.

J. Ellsworth Baker, tout de suite de France, place de naissance Amerique, destination la Grand Bretagne.

I love this sort of people. A lady passenger of ours tells of a fellow-citizen of hers who spent eight weeks in Paris and then returned home and addressed his dearest old bosom friend Herbert as 'M. Er-bare'. He apologized, though, and said, "Pon my soul it is aggravating, but I cahn't help it – I have got so used to speaking nothing but French, my dear Erbare – damme there it goes again!

– got so used to French pronunciation that I cahn't get rid of it – it is positively annoying, I assure you.' This entertaining idiot, whose name was Gordon, allowed himself to be hailed three times in the street before he paid any attention, and then begged a thousand pardons and said he had grown so accustomed to hearing himself addressed as 'M'sieu *Gor-r-dong*', with a roll to the r, that he had forgotten the legitimate sound of his name! He wore a rose in his buttonhole; he gave the French salutation – two flips of the hand in front of the face; he called Paris *Pairree* in ordinary English conversation; he carried envelopes bearing foreign postmarks protruding from his breast-pocket; he cultivated a moustache and imperial, and did what else he could to suggest to the beholder his pet fancy that he resembled Louis Napoleon – and in a spirit of thankfulness which is entirely unaccountable, considering the slim foundation there was for it, he praised his Maker that he was as he was, and went on enjoying his little life just the same as if he really had been deliberately designed and erected by the great Architect of the Universe.

Think of our Whitcombs, and our Ainsworths and our Williamses writing themselves down in dilapidated French in foreign hotel registers! We laugh at Englishmen, when we are at home, for sticking so sturdily to their national ways and customs, but we look back upon it from abroad very forgivingly. It is not pleasant to see an American thrusting his nationality forward obtrusively in a foreign land, but Oh, it is pitiable to see him making of himself a thing that is neither male nor female, neither fish, flesh, nor fowl – a poor, miserable, hermaphrodite Frenchman!

Among a long list of churches, art galleries, and such things, visited by us in Venice, I shall mention only one – the church of Santa Maria dei Frari. It is about 500 years old, I believe, and stands on twelve hundred thousand piles. In it lie the body of Canova and the heart of Titian, under magnificent monuments. Titian died at the age of almost one hundred years. A plague which swept away 50,000 lives was raging at the time, and there is notable evidence of the reverence in which the great painter was held, in the fact that to him alone the state permitted a public funeral in all that season of terror and death.

In this church, also, is a monument to the doge Foscari, whose name a once resident of Venice, Lord Byron, has made permanently famous.

The monument to the doge Giovanni Pesaro, in this church, is a curiosity in the way of mortuary adornment. It is eighty feet high and is fronted like some fantastic pagan temple. Against it stand four colossal Nubians, as black as night, dressed in white marble garments. The black legs are bare, and through rents in sleeves and breeches, the skin, of shiny black marble, shows. The artist was as ingenious as his funeral designs were absurd. There are two bronze skeletons bearing scrolls, and two great dragons uphold the sarcophagus. On high, amid all this grotesqueness, sits the departed doge.

In the conventual buildings attached to this church are the state archives of Venice. We did not see them, but they are said to number millions of documents. 'They are the records of centuries of the most watchful, observant and suspicious government that ever existed – in which everything was written down and nothing spoken out.' They fill nearly 300 rooms. Among them are manuscripts from the archives of nearly 2,000 families, monasteries and convents. The secret history of Venice for a thousand years is here – its plots, its hidden trials, its assassinations, its commissions of hireling spies and masked bravoes – food, ready to hand, for a world of dark and mysterious romances.

Yes, I think we have seen all of Venice. We have seen, in these old churches, a profusion of costly and elaborate sepulchre ornamentation such as we never dreamt of before. We have stood in the dim religious light of these hoary sanctuaries, in the midst of long ranks of dusty monuments and effigies of the great dead of Venice, until we seemed drifting back, back, back, into the solemn past, and looking upon the scenes and mingling with the peoples of a remote antiquity. We have been in a half-waking sort of dream all the time. I do not know how else to describe the feeling. A part of our being has remained still in the nineteenth century, while another part of it has seemed in some unaccountable way walking among the phantoms of the tenth.

We have seen famous pictures until our eyes are weary with looking at them and refuse to find interest in them any longer. And what wonder, when there are 1,200 pictures by Palma the Younger in Venice and 1,500 by Tintoretto? And behold there are Titians and the works of other artists in proportion. We have seen Titian's celebrated Cain and Abel, his David and Goliath, his Abraham's Sacrifice. We have seen Tintoretto's monster picture, which is seventy-four feet long and I do not know how many feet high, and thought it a very commodious picture. We have seen pictures of martyrs enough, and saints enough, to regenerate the world. I ought not to confess it, but still, since one has no opportunity in America to acquire a critical judgment in art, and since I could not hope to become educated in it in Europe in a few short weeks, I may therefore as well acknowledge with such apologies as may be due, that to me it seemed that when I had seen one of these martyrs I had seen them all. They all have a marked family resemblance to each other, they dress alike, in coarse monkish robes and sandals, they are all bald headed, they all stand in about the same attitude, and without exception they are gazing heavenward with countenances which the Ainsworths, the Mortons and the Williamses, *et fils*, inform me are full of 'expression'. To me there is nothing tangible about these imaginary portraits, nothing that I can grasp and take a living interest in. If great Titian had only been gifted with prophecy, and had skipped a martyr, and gone over to England and painted a portrait of Shakspeare, even as a youth, which we could all have confidence in now, the world down to the latest generations would have forgiven him the lost martyr in the rescued seer. I think posterity could have spared one more martyr for the sake of a great historical picture of Titian's time and painted by his brush – such as Columbus returning in chains from the discovery of a world, for instance. The old masters did paint some Venetian historical pictures, and these we did not tire of looking at, notwithstanding representations of the formal introduction of defunct doges to the Virgin Mary in regions beyond the clouds clashed rather harshly with the proprieties, it seemed to us.

But humble as we are, and unpretending, in the matter of art, our researches among the painted monks and martyrs have not been wholly in vain. We have striven hard to learn. We have had some success. We have mastered some things, possibly of trifling import in the eyes of the learned, but to us they give pleasure, and we take as much pride in our little acquirements as do others who have learned far more, and we love to display them full as well. When we see a monk going about with a lion and looking tranquilly up to heaven, we know that that is St Mark. When we see a monk with a book and a pen, looking tranquilly up to heaven, trying to think of a word, we know that that is St Matthew. When we see a monk sitting on a rock, looking tranquilly up to heaven, with a human skull beside him, and without other baggage, we know that that is St Jerome. Because we know that he always went flying light in the matter of baggage. When we see a party looking tranquilly up to heaven, unconscious that his body is shot through and through with arrows, we know that that is St Sebastian. When we see other monks looking tranquilly up to heaven, but having no trademark, we always ask who those parties are. We do this because we humbly wish to learn. We have seen 13,000 St Jeromes, and 22,000 St Marks, and sixteen thousand St Matthews, and 60,000 St Sebastians, and four millions of assorted monks, undesignated, and we feel encouraged to believe that when we have seen some more of these various pictures, and had a larger experience, we shall begin to take an absorbing interest in them like our cultivated countrymen from Amerique.

Now it does give me real pain to speak in this almost unappreciative way of the old masters and their martyrs, because good friends of mine in the ship – friends who do thoroughly and conscientiously appreciate them and are in every way competent to discriminate between good pictures and inferior ones – have urged me for my own sake not to make public the fact that I lack this appreciation and this critical discrimination myself. I believe that what I have written and may still write about pictures will give them pain, and I am honestly sorry for it. I even promised that I would hide my uncouth sentiments in my own breast. But alas! I never could keep a promise. I do not blame myself for this weakness, because the fault must lie in my physical organization. It is likely that such a very liberal amount of space was given to the organ which enables me to make promises, that the organ which should enable me to keep them was crowded out. But I grieve not. I like no half-way things. I had rather have one faculty nobly developed than two faculties of mere ordinary capacity. I certainly meant to keep that promise, but I find I cannot do it. It is impossible to travel through Italy without speaking of pictures, and can I see them through others' eyes?

If I did not so delight in the grand pictures that are spread before me every day of my life by that monarch of all the old masters, Nature, I should come to believe, sometimes, that I had in me no appreciation of the beautiful, whatsoever.

It seems to me that whenever I glory to think that for once I have discovered an ancient painting that is beautiful and worthy of all praise, the pleasure it gives me is an infallible proof that it is not a beautiful picture and not in any wise worthy of commendation. This very thing has occurred more times than I can mention, in Venice. In every single instance the guide has crushed out my swelling enthusiasm with the remark:

'It is nothing – it is of the *Renaissance*.'

I did not know what in the mischief the Renaissance was, and so always I had to simply say,

'Ah! so it is – I had not observed it before.'

I could not bear to be ignorant before a cultivated negro, the offspring of a South Carolina slave. But it occurred too often for even my self-complacency, did that exasperating 'It is nothing – it is of the *Renaissance*.' *I* said at last:

'Who is this *Renaissance*? Where did he come from? Who gave him permission to cram the Republic with his execrable daubs?'

We learned, then, that Renaissance was not a man; that *renaissance* was a term used to signify what was at best but an imperfect rejuvenation of art. The guide said that after Titian's time and the time of the other great names we had grown so familiar with, high art declined; then it partially rose again – an inferior sort of painters sprang up, and these shabby pictures were the work of their hands. Then I said, in my heat, that I 'wished to goodness high art had declined 500 years sooner'. The Renaissance pictures suit me very well, though sooth to say its school were too much given to painting real men and did not indulge enough in martyrs.

The guide I have spoken of is the only one we have had yet who knew anything. He was born in South Carolina, of slave parents. They came to Venice while he was an infant. He has grown up here. He is well educated. He reads, writes, and speaks English, Italian, Spanish, and French, with perfect facility; is a worshipper of art and thoroughly conversant with it; knows the history of Venice by heart and never tires of talking of her illustrious career. He dresses better than any of us, I think, and is daintily polite. Negroes are deemed as good as white people, in Venice, and so this man feels no desire to go back to his native land. His judgment is correct.

❧

I have had another shave. I was writing in our front room this afternoon and trying hard to keep my attention on my work and refrain from looking out upon the canal. I was resisting the soft influences of the climate as well as I could, and endeavoring to overcome the desire to be indolent and happy. The boys sent for a barber. They asked me if I would be shaved. I reminded them of my tortures in Genoa, Milan, Como; of my declaration that I would suffer no more on Italian soil. I said 'Not any for me, if you please.'

I wrote on. The barber began on the doctor. I heard him say:

'Dan, this is the easiest shave I have had since we left the ship.'

He said again, presently:

'Why Dan, a man could go to sleep with this man shaving him.'

Dan took the chair. Then he said:

'Why this is Titian. This is one of the old masters.'

I wrote on. Directly Dan said:

'Doctor, it is perfect luxury. The ship's barber isn't anything to him.'

My rough beard wee distressing me beyond measure. The barber was rolling up his apparatus. The temptation was too strong. I said:

'Hold on, please. Shave me also.'

I sat down in the chair and closed my eyes. The barber soaped my face, and then took his razor and gave me a rake that well nigh threw me into convulsions. I jumped out of the chair: Dan and the doctor were both wiping blood off their faces and laughing.

I said it was a mean, disgraceful fraud.

They said that the misery of this shave had gone so far beyond anything they had ever experienced before, that they could not bear the idea of losing such a chance of hearing a cordial opinion from me on the subject.

It was shameful. But there was no help for it. The skinning was begun and had to be finished. The tears flowed with every rake, and so did the fervent execrations. The barber grew confused, and brought blood every time. I think the boys enjoyed it better than anything they have seen or heard since they left home.

We have seen the Campanile, and Byron's house and Balbi's the geographer, and the palaces of all the ancient dukes and doges of Venice, and we have seen their effeminate descendants airing their nobility in fashionable French attire in the Grand Square of St Mark, and eating ices and drinking cheap wines, instead of wearing gallant coats of mail and destroying fleets and armies as their great ancestors did in the days of Venetian glory. We have seen no bravoes with poisoned stilettos, no masks, no wild carnival; but we have seen the ancient pride of Venice, the grim Bronze Horses that figure in a thousand legends. Venice may well cherish them, for they are the only horses she ever had. It is said there are hundreds of people in this curious city who never have seen a living horse in their lives.

It is entirely true, no doubt.

And so, having satisfied ourselves, we depart tomorrow, and leave the venerable Queen of the Republics to summon her vanished ships, and marshal her shadowy armies, and know again in dreams the pride of her old renown.

❦

There are a good many things about this Italy which I do not understand – and more especially I cannot understand how a bankrupt Government can have such palatial railroad depots and such marvels of turnpikes. Why, these latter are as hard as adamant, as straight as a line, as smooth as a floor, and as white as snow. When it is too dark to see any other object, one can still see the white turnpikes of France and Italy; and they are clean enough to eat from, without a tablecloth. And yet no tolls are charged.

As for the railways – we have none like them. The cars slide as smoothly along as if they were on runners. The depots are vast palaces of cut marble, with stately colonnades of the same royal stone traversing them from end to end, and with ample walls and ceilings richly decorated with frescoes. The lofty gateways are graced with statues, and the broad floors are all laid in polished flags of marble.

These things win me more than Italy's hundred galleries of priceless art treasures, because I can understand the one and am not competent to appreciate the other. In the turnpikes, the railways, the depots, and the new boulevards of uniform houses in Florence and other cities here, I see the genius of Louis Napoleon, or rather, I see the works of that statesman imitated. But Louis has taken care that in France there shall be a foundation for these improvements – money. He has always the wherewithal to back up his projects; they strengthen France and never weaken her. Her material prosperity is genuine. But here the case is different. This country is bankrupt. There is no real foundation for these great works. The prosperity they would seem to indicate is a pretence. There is no money in the treasury, and so they enfeeble her instead of strengthening. Italy has achieved the dearest wish of her heart and become an independent State – and in so doing she has drawn an elephant in the political lottery. She has nothing to feed it on. Inexperienced in government, she plunged into all manner of useless expenditure, and swamped her treasury almost in a day. She squandered millions of francs on a navy which she did not need, and the first time she took her new toy into action she got it knocked higher than Gilderoy's kite – to use the language of the Pilgrims.

But it is an ill-wind that blows nobody good. A year ago, when Italy saw utter ruin staring her in the face and her greenbacks hardly worth the paper they were printed on, her Parliament ventured upon a 'coup de main' that would have appalled the stoutest of her statesmen under less desperate circumstances. They, in a manner, confiscated the domains of the Church! This in priest-ridden Italy! This in a land which has groped in the midnight of priestly superstition for 1,600 years! It was a rare good fortune for Italy, the stress of weather that drove her to break from this prison-house.

They do not call it *confiscating* the church property. That would sound too harshly yet. But it amounts to that. There are thousands of churches in Italy, each with untold millions of treasures stored away in its closets, and each with its battalion of priests to be supported. And then there are the estates of the Church – league on league of the richest lands and the noblest forests in all Italy – all yielding immense revenues to the Church, and none paying a cent in taxes to the State. In some great districts the Church owns *all* the property – lands, watercourses, woods, mills and factories. They buy, they sell, they manufacture, and since they pay no taxes, who can hope to compete with them?

Well, the Government has seized all this in effect, and will yet seize it in rigid and unpoetical reality, no doubt. Something must be done to feed a starving treasury, and there is no other resource in all Italy – none but the riches of the Church. So the Government intends to take to itself a great portion of the revenues arising from priestly farms, factories, etc., and also intends to take possession of the churches and carry them on, after its own fashion and upon its own responsibility. In a few instances it will leave the establishments of great pet churches undisturbed, but in all others only a handful of priests will be retained to preach and pray, a few will be pensioned, and the balance turned adrift.

Pray glance at some of these churches and their embellishments, and see whether the Government is doing a righteous thing or not. In Venice, today, a city of a 100,000 inhabitants, there are 1,200 priests. Heaven only knows how many there were before the Parliament reduced their numbers. There was the great Jesuit Church. Under the old regime it required sixty priests to engineer it – the Government does it with five, now, and the others are discharged from service. All about that church wretchedness and poverty abound. At its door a dozen hats and bonnets were doffed to us, as many heads were humbly bowed, and as many hands extended, appealing for pennies – appealing with foreign words we could not understand, but appealing mutely, with sad eyes, and sunken cheeks, and ragged raiment, that no words were needed to translate. Then we passed within the great doors, and it seemed that the riches of the world were before us! Huge columns carved out of single masses of marble, and inlaid from top to bottom with a hundred intricate figures wrought in costly verde antique; pulpits of the same rich materials, whose draperies hung down in many a pictured fold, the stony fabric counterfeiting the delicate work of the loom; the grand altar brilliant with polished facings and balustrades of oriental agate, jasper, verde antique, and other precious stones, whose names, even, we seldom hear – and slabs of priceless lapis lazuli lavished everywhere as recklessly as if the church had owned a quarry of it. In the midst of all this magnificence, the solid gold and silver furniture of the altar seemed cheap and trivial. Even the floors and ceilings cost a princely fortune.

Now, where is the use of allowing all those riches to lie idle, while half of that community hardly know, from day to day, how they are going to keep body and soul together? And, where is the wisdom in permitting hundreds upon hundreds of millions of francs to be locked up in the useless trumpery of churches all over Italy, and the people ground to death with taxation to uphold a perishing Government?

As far as I can see, Italy, for 1,500 years, has turned all her energies, all her finances, and all her industry to the building up of a vast array of wonderful church edifices, and starving half her citizens to accomplish it. She is today one vast museum of magnificence and misery. All the churches in an ordinary American city put together could hardly buy the jeweled frippery in one of her hundred cathedrals. And for every beggar in America, Italy can show a hundred – and rags and vermin to match. It is the wretchedest, princeliest land on earth.

Look at the grand Duomo of Florence – a vast pile that has been sapping the purses of her citizens for 500 years, and is not nearly finished yet. Like all other men, I fell down and worshipped it, but when the filthy beggars swarmed around me the contrast was too striking, too suggestive, and I said, 'O, sons of classic Italy, *is* the spirit of enterprise, of self-reliance, of noble endeavor, utterly dead within ye? Curse your indolent worthlessness, why don't you rob your church?'

Three hundred happy, comfortable priests are employed in that Cathedral.

And now that my temper is up, I may as well go on and abuse everybody I can think of. They have a grand mausoleum in Florence, which they built to bury our Lord and Saviour and the Medici family in. It sounds blasphemous, but it is true, and here they *act* blasphemy. The dead and damned Medicis who cruelly tyrannized over Florence and were her curse for over 200 years, are salted away in a circle of costly vaults, and in their midst the Holy Sepulchre was to have been set up. The expedition sent to Jerusalem to seize it got into trouble and could not accomplish the burglary, and so the center of the mausoleum is vacant now. They say the entire mausoleum was intended for the Holy Sepulchre, and was only turned into a family burying place after the Jerusalem expedition failed – but you will excuse me. Some of those Medicis would have smuggled themselves in sure. – What *they* had not the effrontery to do, was not worth doing. Why, they had their trivial, forgotten exploits on land and sea pictured out in grand frescoes (as did also the ancient Doges of Venice) with the Saviour and the Virgin throwing bouquets to them out of the clouds, and the Deity himself applauding from his throne in Heaven! And who painted these things? Why, Titian, Tintoretto, Paul Veronese, Raphael – none other than the world's idols, the 'old masters'.

Andrea del Sarto glorified his princes in pictures that must save them forever from the oblivion they merited, and they let him starve. Served him right. Raphael pictured such infernal villains as Catherine and Marie de Medicis seated in heaven and conversing familiarly with the Virgin Mary and the angels, (to say nothing of higher personages) and yet my friends abuse me because I am a little prejudiced against the old masters – because I fail sometimes to see the beauty that is in their productions. I cannot help but see it, now and then, but I keep on protesting against the groveling spirit that could persuade those masters to prostitute their noble talents to the adulation of such monsters as the French, Venetian and Florentine Princes of 200 and 300 years ago, all the same.

I am told that the old masters had to do these shameful things for bread, the princes and potentates being the only patrons of art. If a grandly gifted man may drag his pride and his manhood in the dirt for bread rather than starve with the nobility that is in him untainted, the excuse is a valid one. It would excuse theft in Washingtons and Wellingtons, and unchastity in women as well.

But somehow, I cannot keep that Medici mausoleum out of my memory. It is as large as a church; its pavement is rich enough for the pavement of a King's palace; its great dome is gorgeous with frescoes; its walls are made of – what? Marble? – plaster? – wood? – paper? No. Red porphyry – verde antique – jasper – oriental agate – alabaster – mother-of-pearl – chalcedony – red coral – lapis lazuli! All the vast walls are made wholly of these precious stones, worked in, and in and in together in elaborate patterns and figures, and polished till they glow like great mirrors with the pictured splendors reflected from the dome overhead. And before a statue of one of those dead Medicis reposes a crown that blazes with diamonds and emeralds enough to buy a ship-of-the-line, almost. These are the things the Government has its evil eye upon, and a happy thing it will be for Italy when they melt away in the public treasury.

And now – However, another beggar approaches. I will go out and destroy him, and then come back and write another chapter of vituperation.

Having eaten the friendless orphan – having driven away his comrades – having grown calm and reflective at length – I now feel in a kindlier mood. I feel that after talking so freely about the priests and the churches, justice demands that if I know anything good about either I ought to say it. I *have* heard of many things that redound to the credit of the priesthood, but the most notable matter that occurs to me now is the devotion one of the mendicant orders showed during the prevalence of the cholera last year. I speak of the Dominican friars – men who wear a coarse, heavy brown robe and a cowl, in this hot climate, and go barefoot. They live on alms altogether, I believe. They must unquestionably love their religion, to suffer so much for it. When the cholera was raging in Naples; when the people were dying by hundreds and hundreds every day; when every concern for the public welfare was swallowed up in selfish private interest, and every citizen made the taking care of himself his sole object, these men banded themselves together and went about nursing the sick and burying the dead. Their noble efforts cost many of them their lives. They laid them down cheerfully, and well they might. Creeds mathematically precise, and hair-splitting niceties of doctrine, are absolutely necessary for the salvation of some kinds of souls, but surely the charity, the purity, the unselfishness that are in the hearts of men like these would save their souls though they were bankrupt in the true religion – which is ours.

One of these fat bare-footed rascals came here to Civita Vecchia with us in the little French steamer. There were only half a dozen of us in the cabin. He belonged in the steerage. He was the life of the ship, the bloody-minded son of the Inquisition! He and the leader of the marine band of a French man-of-war played on the piano and sang opera turn about; they sang duets together; they rigged impromptu theatrical costumes and gave us extravagant farces and pantomimes. We got along first-rate with the friar, and were excessively conversational, albeit he could not understand what we said, and certainly he never uttered a word that we could guess the meaning of.

This Civita Vecchia is the finest nest of dirt, vermin and ignorance we have found yet, except that African perdition they call Tangier, which is just like it. The people here live in alleys two yards wide, which have a smell about them which is peculiar but not entertaining. It is well the alleys are not wider, because they hold as much smell now as a person can stand, and of course, if they were wider they would hold more, and then the people would die. These alleys are paved with stone, and carpeted with deceased cats, and decayed rags, and decomposed vegetable-tops, and remnants of old boots, all soaked with dishwater, and the people sit around on stools and enjoy it. They are indolent, as a general thing, and yet have few pastimes. They work two or three hours at a time, but not hard, and then they knock off and catch flies. This does not require any talent, because they only have to grab – if they do not get the one they are after, they get another. It is all the same to them. They have no partialities. Whichever one they get is the one they want.

They have other kinds of insects, but it does not make them arrogant. They are very quiet, unpretending people. They have more of these kind of things than other communities, but they do not boast.

They are very uncleanly – these people – in face, in person and dress. When they see anybody with a clean shirt on, it arouses their scorn. The women wash clothes, half the day, at the public tanks in the streets, but they are probably somebody else's. Or maybe they keep one set to wear and another to wash; because they never put on any that have ever been washed. When they get done washing, they sit in the alleys and nurse their cubs. They nurse one ash-cat at a time, and the others scratch their backs against the doorpost and are happy.

All this country belongs to the Papal States. They do not appear to have any schools here, and only one billiard table. Their education is at a very low stage. One portion of the men go into the military, another into the priesthood, and the rest into the shoe-making business.

They keep up the passport system here, but so they do in Turkey. This shows that the Papal States are as far advanced as Turkey. This fact will be alone sufficient to silence the tongues of malignant calumniators. I had to get my passport *viséd* for Rome in Florence, and then they would not let me come ashore here until a policeman had examined it on the wharf and sent me a permit. They did not even dare to let me take my passport in my hands for twelve hours, I looked so formidable. They judged it best to let me cool down. They thought I wanted to take the town, likely. Little did they know me. I wouldn't have it. They examined my baggage at the depot. They took one of my ablest jokes and read it over carefully twice and then read it backwards. But it was too deep for them. They passed it around, and everybody speculated on it awhile, but it mastered them all.

It was no common joke. At length a veteran officer spelled it over deliberately and shook his head three or four times and said that in his opinion it was seditious. That was the first time I felt alarmed. I immediately said I would explain the document, and they crowded around. And so I explained and explained and explained, and they took notes of all I said, but the more I explained the more they could not understand it, and when they desisted at last, I could not even understand it myself.

They said they believed it was an incendiary document, leveled at the government. I declared solemnly that it was not, but they only shook their heads and would not be satisfied. Then they consulted a good while; and finally they confiscated it. I was very sorry for this, because I had worked a long time on that joke, and took a good deal of pride in it, and now I suppose I shall never see it any more. I suppose it will be sent up and filed away among the criminal archives of Rome, and will always be regarded as a mysterious infernal machine which would have blown up like a mine and scattered the good Pope all around, but for a miraculous providential interference. And I suppose that all the time I am in Rome the police will dog me about from place to place because they think I am a dangerous character.

It is fearfully hot in Civita Vecchia. The streets are made very narrow and the houses built very solid and heavy and high, as a protection against the heat. This is the first Italian town I have seen which does not appear to have a patron saint. I suppose no saint but the one that went up in the chariot of fire could stand the climate.

There is nothing here to see. They have not even a cathedral, with eleven tons of solid silver archbishops in the back room; and they do not show you any moldy buildings that are 7,000 years old; nor any smoke-dried old fire-screens which are *chef d'oeuvres* of Reubens or Simpson, or Titian or Ferguson, or any of those parties; and they haven't any bottled fragments of saints, and not even a nail from the true cross. We are going to Rome. There is nothing to see here.

In this connection I wish to say one word about Michael Angelo Buonarotti. I used to worship the mighty genius of Michael Angelo – that man who was great in poetry, painting, sculpture, architecture – great in everything he undertook. But I do not want Michael Angelo for breakfast – for luncheon – for dinner – for tea – for supper – for between meals. I like a change, occasionally. In Genoa, he designed everything; in Milan he or his pupils designed everything; he designed the Lake of Como; in Padua, Verona, Venice, Bologna, who did we ever hear of, from guides, but Michael Angelo? In Florence, he painted everything, designed everything, nearly, and what he did not design he used to sit on a favorite stone and look at, and they showed us the stone. In Pisa he designed everything but the old shot-tower, and they would have attributed that to him if it had not been so awfully out of the perpendicular. He designed the piers of Leghorn and the custom house regulations of Civita Vecchia. But, here – here it is frightful. He designed St Peter's; he designed the Pope; he designed the Pantheon, the uniform of the Pope's soldiers, the Tiber, the Vatican, the Coliseum, the Capitol, the Tarpeian Rock, the Barberini Palace, St John Lateran, the Campagna, the Appian Way, the Seven Hills, the Baths of Caracalla, the Claudian Aqueduct, the Cloaca Maxima – the eternal bore designed the Eternal City, and unless all men and books do lie, he painted everything in it! Dan said the other day to the guide, 'Enough, enough, enough! Say no more! Lump the whole thing! say that the Creator made Italy from designs by Michael Angelo!'

I never felt so fervently thankful, so soothed, so tranquil, so filled with a blessed peace, as I did yesterday when I learned that Michael Angelo was dead.

But we have taken it out of this guide. He has marched us through miles of pictures and sculpture in the vast corridors of the Vatican; and through miles of pictures and sculpture in twenty other palaces; he has shown us the great picture in the Sistine Chapel, and frescoes enough to frescoe the heavens – pretty much all done by Michael Angelo. So with him we have played that game which has vanquished so many guides for us – imbecility and idiotic questions. These creatures never suspect – they have no idea of a sarcasm.

He shows us a figure and says: 'Statoo brunzo.' (Bronze statue.)
We look at it indifferently and the doctor asks: 'Michael Angelo?'
'No – not know who.'

Then he shows us the ancient Roman Forum. The doctor asks: 'Michael Angelo?'

A stare from the guide. 'No – thousan' year before he is born.'

Then an Egyptian obelisk. Again: 'Michael Angelo?'

'Oh, *mon dieu*, genteelmen! Zis is *two* thousan' year before he is born!'

He grows so tired of that unceasing question sometimes, that he dreads to show us anything at all. The wretch has tried all the ways he can think of to make us comprehend that Michael Angelo is only responsible for the creation of a part of the world, but somehow he has not succeeded yet. Relief for overtasked eyes and brain from study and sightseeing is necessary, or we shall become idiotic sure enough. Therefore this guide must continue to suffer. If he does not enjoy it, so much the worse for him. We do.

In this place I may as well jot down a chapter concerning those necessary nuisances, European guides. Many a man has wished in his heart he could do without his guide; but knowing he could not, has wished he could get some amusement out of him as a remuneration for the affliction of his society. We accomplished this latter matter, and if our experience can be made useful to others they are welcome to it.

Guides know about enough English to tangle everything up so that a man can make neither head or tail of it. They know their story by heart – the history of every statue, painting, cathedral or other wonder they show you. They know it and tell it as a parrot would – and if you interrupt, and throw them off the track, they have to go back and begin over again. All their lives long, they are employed in showing strange things to foreigners and listening to their bursts of admiration. It is human nature to take delight in exciting admiration. It is what prompts children to say 'smart' things, and do absurd ones, and in other ways 'show off' when company is present. It is what makes gossips turn out in rain and storm to go and be the first to tell a startling bit of news. Think, then, what a passion it becomes with a guide, whose privilege it is, every day, to show to strangers wonders that throw them into perfect ecstasies of admiration! He gets so that he could not by any possibility live in a soberer atmosphere. After we discovered this, we *never* went into ecstasies any more – we never admired anything – we never showed any but impassible faces and stupid indifference in the presence of the sublimest wonders a guide had to display. We had found their weak point. We have made good use of it ever since. We have made some of those people savage, at times, but we have never lost our own serenity.

The doctor asks the questions, generally, because he can keep his countenance, and look more like an inspired idiot, and throw more imbecility into the tone of his voice than any man that lives. It comes natural to him.

The guides in Genoa are delighted to secure an American party, because Americans so much wonder, and deal so much in sentiment and emotion before any relic of Columbus. Our guide there fidgeted about as if he had swallowed a spring mattress. He was full of animation – full of impatience. He said:

'Come wis me, genteelmen! – come! I show you ze letter writing by Christopher Colombo! – write it himself! – write it wis his own hand! – come!'

He took us to the municipal palace. After much impressive fumbling of keys and opening of locks, the stained and aged document was spread before us. The guide's eyes sparkled. He danced about us and tapped the parchment with his finger:

'What I tell you, genteelmen! Is it not so? See! handwriting Christopher Colombo! – write it himself!'

We looked indifferent – unconcerned. The doctor examined the document very deliberately, during a painful pause. – Then he said, without any show of interest:

'Ah – Ferguson – what – what did you say was the name of the party who wrote this?'

'Christopher Colombo! ze great Christopher Colombo!'

Another deliberate examination.

'Ah – did he write it himself; or – or how?'

'He write it himself! – Christopher Colombo! He's own hand-writing, write by himself!'

Then the doctor laid the document down and said:

'Why, I have seen boys in America only fourteen years old that could write better than that.'

'But zis is ze great Christo –'

'I don't care who it is! It's the worst writing I ever saw. Now you musn't think you can impose on us because we are strangers. We are not fools, by a good deal. If you have got any specimens of penmanship of real merit, trot them out! – and if you haven't, drive on!'

We drove on. The guide was considerably shaken up, but he made one more venture. He had something which he thought would overcome us. He said:

'Ah, genteelmen, you come wis me! I show you beautiful, O, magnificent bust Christopher Colombo! – splendid, grand, magnificent!'

He brought us before the beautiful bust--for it was beautiful--and sprang back and struck an attitude:

'Ah, look, genteelmen! – beautiful, grand, – bust Christopher Colombo! – beautiful bust, beautiful pedestal!'

The doctor put up his eye-glass – procured for such occasions:

'Ah – what did you say this gentleman's name was?'

'Christopher Colombo! – ze great Christopher Colombo!'

'Christopher Colombo – the great Christopher Colombo. Well, what did he do?'

'Discover America! – discover America, Oh, ze devil!'

'Discover America. No – that statement will hardly wash. We are just from America ourselves. We heard nothing about it. Christopher Colombo – pleasant name – is – is he dead?'

'Oh, corpo di Baccho! – three hundred year!'

'What did he die of?'

'I do not know! – I can not tell.'

'Smallpox, think?'

'I do not know, genteelmen! – I do not know *what* he die of!'

'Measles, likely?'

'May be – may be – I do *not* know – I think he die of somethings.'

'Parents living?'

'Im-poseeeble!'

'Ah – which is the bust and which is the pedestal?'

'Santa Maria! – zis ze bust! – zis ze pedestal!'

'Ah, I see, I see – happy combination – very happy combination, indeed. Is – is this the first time this gentleman was ever on a bust?'

That joke was lost on the foreigner – guides cannot master the subtleties of the American joke.

We have made it interesting for this Roman guide. Yesterday we spent three or four hours in the Vatican, again, that wonderful world of curiosities. We came very near expressing interest, sometimes – even admiration – it was very hard to keep from it. We succeeded though. Nobody else ever did, in the Vatican museums. The guide was bewildered – nonplussed. He walked his legs off, nearly, hunting up extraordinary things, and exhausted all his ingenuity on us, but it was a failure; we never showed any interest in anything. He had reserved what he considered to be his greatest wonder till the last – a royal Egyptian mummy, the best preserved in the world, perhaps. He took us there. He felt so sure, this time, that some of his old enthusiasm came back to him:

'See, genteelmen! – Mummy! Mummy!'

The eye-glass came up as calmly, as deliberately as ever.

'Ah, – Ferguson – what did I understand you to say the gentleman's name was?'

'Name? – he got no name! – Mummy! '*Gyptian* mummy!'

'Yes, yes. Born here?'

'No! 'Gyptian mummy!'

'Ah, just so. Frenchman, I presume?'

'No! – *not* Frenchman, not Roman! – born in Egypta!'

'Born in Egypta. Never heard of Egypta before. Foreign locality, likely. Mummy – mummy. How calm he is – how self-possessed. Is, ah – is he dead?'

'Oh, *sacré bleu*, been dead three thousan' year!'

The doctor turned on him savagely:

'Here, now, what do you mean by such conduct as this! Playing us for Chinamen because we are strangers and trying to learn! Trying to impose your vile second-hand carcasses on *us*! – thunder and lightning, I've a notion to – to – if you've got a nice *fresh* corpse, fetch him out! – or by George we'll brain you!'

We make it exceedingly interesting for this Frenchman. However, he has paid us back, partly, without knowing it. He came to the hotel this morning to ask if we were up, and he endeavored as well as he could to describe us, so that the landlord would know which persons he meant. He finished with the casual remark that we were lunatics. The observation was so innocent and so honest that it amounted to a very good thing for a guide to say.

There is one remark (already mentioned) which never yet has failed to disgust these guides. We use it always, when we can think of nothing else to say. After they have exhausted their enthusiasm pointing out to us and praising the beauties of some ancient bronze image or broken-legged statue, we look at it stupidly and in silence for five, ten, fifteen minutes – as long as we can hold out, in fact – and then ask:

'Is – is he dead?'

That conquers the serenest of them. It is not what they are looking for – especially a new guide. Our Roman Ferguson is the most patient, unsuspecting, long-suffering subject we have had yet. We shall be sorry to part with him. We have enjoyed his society very much. We trust he has enjoyed ours, but we are harassed with doubts.

᪥

They pronounce it Pom-pay-e. I always had an idea that you went down into Pompeii with torches, by the way of damp, dark stairways, just as you do in silver mines, and traversed gloomy tunnels with lava overhead and something on either hand like dilapidated prisons gouged out of the solid earth, that faintly resembled houses. But you do nothing the kind. Fully one-half of the buried city, perhaps, is completely exhumed and thrown open freely to the light of day; and there stand the long rows of solidly-built brick houses (roofless) just as they stood 1,800 years ago, hot with the flaming sun; and there lie their floors, clean-swept, and not a bright fragment tarnished or waiting of the labored mosaics that pictured them with the beasts, and birds, and flowers which we copy in perishable carpets today; and here are the Venuses, and Bacchuses, and Adonises, making love and getting drunk in many-hued frescoes on the walls of saloon and bedchamber; and there are the narrow streets and narrower sidewalks, paved with flags of good hard lava, the one deeply rutted with the chariot-wheels, and the other with the passing feet of the Pompeiians of bygone centuries; and there are the bake-shops, the temples, the halls of justice, the baths, the theaters – all clean-scraped and neat, and suggesting nothing of the nature of a silver mine away down in the bowels of the earth. The broken pillars lying about, the doorless doorways and the crumbled tops of the wilderness of walls, were wonderfully suggestive of the 'burnt district' in one of our cities, and if there had been any charred timbers, shattered windows, heaps of debris, and general blackness and smokiness about the place, the resemblance would have been perfect. But no – the sun shines as brightly down on old Pompeii today as it did when Christ was born in Bethlehem, and its streets are cleaner a hundred times than ever Pompeiian saw them in her prime. I know whereof I speak – for in the great, chief thoroughfares (Merchant Street and the Street of Fortune) have I not seen with my own eyes how 200 years at least the pavements were not repaired! – how ruts five and even ten inches deep were worn into the thick flagstones by the chariot-wheels of generations of swindled tax-payers? And do I not know by these signs that Street Commissioners of Pompeii never attended to their business, and that if they never mended the pavements they never cleaned them? And, besides, is it not the inborn nature of Street Commissioners to avoid their duty whenever they get a chance? I wish I knew the name of the last one that held office in Pompeii so that I could give him a blast. I speak with feeling on this subject, because I caught my foot in one of those ruts, and the sadness that came over me when I saw the first poor skeleton, with ashes and lava sticking to it, was tempered by the reflection that may be that party was the Street Commissioner.

No – Pompeii is no longer a buried city. It is a city of hundreds and hundreds of roofless houses, and a tangled maze of streets where one could easily get lost, without a guide, and have to sleep in some ghostly palace that had known no living tenant since that awful November night of eighteen centuries ago.

We passed through the gate which faces the Mediterranean, (called the Marine Gate,) and by the rusty, broken image of

Minerva, still keeping tireless watch and ward over the possessions it was powerless to save, and went up a long street and stood in the broad court of the Forum of Justice. The floor was level and clean, and up and down either side was a noble colonnade of broken pillars, with their beautiful Ionic and Corinthian columns scattered about them. At the upper end were the vacant seats of the Judges, and behind them we descended into a dungeon where the ashes and cinders had found two prisoners chained on that memorable November night, and tortured them to death. How they must have tugged at the pitiless fetters as the fierce fires surged around them!

Then we lounged through many and many a sumptuous private mansion which we could not have entered without a formal invitation in incomprehensible Latin, in the olden time, when the owners lived there – and we probably wouldn't have got it. These people built their houses a good deal alike. The floors were laid in fanciful figures wrought in mosaics of many-colored marbles. At the threshold your eyes fall upon a Latin sentence of welcome, sometimes, or a picture of a dog, with the legend 'Beware of the Dog,' and sometimes a picture of a bear or a faun with no inscription at all. Then you enter a sort of vestibule, where they used to keep the hat-rack, I suppose; next a room with a large marble basin in the midst and the pipes of a fountain; on either side are bedrooms; beyond the fountain is a reception-room, then a little garden, dining-room, and so forth and so on. The floors were all mosaic, the walls were stuccoed, or frescoed, or ornamented with bas-reliefs, and here and there were statues, large and small, and little fish-pools, and cascades of sparkling water that sprang from secret places in the colonnade of handsome pillars that surrounded the court, and kept the flowerbeds fresh and the air cool. Those Pompeiians were very luxurious in their tastes and habits. The most exquisite bronzes we have seen in Europe, came from the exhumed cities of Herculaneum and Pompeii, and also the finest cameos and the most delicate engravings on precious stones; their pictures, eighteen or nineteen centuries old, are often much more pleasing than the celebrated rubbish of the old masters of three centuries ago. They were well up in art. From the creation of these works of the first, clear up to the eleventh century, art seems hardly to have existed at all – at least no remnants of it are left – and it was curious to see how far (in some things, at any rate,) these old time pagans excelled the remote generations of masters that came after them. The pride of the world in sculptures seem to be the Laocoon and the Dying Gladiator, in Rome. They are as old as Pompeii, were dug from the earth like Pompeii; but their exact age or who made them can only be conjectured. But worn, and cracked, without a history, and with the blemishing stains of numberless centuries upon them, they still mutely mock at all efforts to rival their perfections.

It was a quaint and curious pastime, wandering through this old silent city of the dead – lounging through utterly deserted streets where thousands and thousands of human beings once bought and sold, and walked and rode, and made the place resound with the noise and confusion of traffic and pleasure. They were not lazy. They hurried in those days. We had evidence of that. There was a temple on one corner, and it was a shorter cut to go between the columns of that temple from one street to the other than to go around – and behold that pathway had been worn deep into the heavy flagstone floor of the building by generations of time-saving feet! They would not go around when it was quicker to go through. We do that way in our cities.

Everywhere, you see things that make you wonder how old these old houses were before the night of destruction came – things, too, which bring back those long dead inhabitants and place the living before your eyes. For instance: the steps (two feet thick – lava blocks) that lead up out of the school, and the same kind of steps that lead up into the dress circle of the principal theater, are almost worn through! For ages the boys hurried out of that school, and for ages their parents hurried into that theater, and the nervous feet that have been dust and ashes for eighteen centuries have left their record for us to read today. I imagined I could see crowds of gentlemen and ladies thronging into the theater, with tickets for secured seats in their hands, and on the wall, I read the imaginary placard, in infamous grammar, '*Positively No Free List, Except Members Of The Press!*' Hanging about the doorway (I fancied) were slouchy Pompeiian street-boys uttering slang and profanity, and keeping a wary eye out for checks. I entered the theater, and sat down in one of the long rows of stone benches in the dress circle, and looked at the place for the orchestra, and the ruined stage, and around at the wide sweep of empty boxes, and thought to myself, 'This house won't pay.' I tried to imagine the music in full blast, the leader of the orchestra beating time, and the 'versatile' So-and-So (who had 'just returned from a most successful tour in the provinces to play his last and farewell engagement of positively six nights only, in Pompeii, previous to his departure for Herculaneum') charging around the stage and piling the agony mountains high – but I could not do it with such a 'house' as that; those empty benches tied my fancy down to dull reality. I said, these people that ought to be here have been dead, and still, and moldering to dust for ages and ages, and will never care for the trifles and follies of life any more for ever – 'Owing to circumstances, etc., etc., there will not be any performance tonight.' Close down the curtain. Put out the lights.

And so I turned away and went through shop after shop and store after store, far down the long street of the merchants, and called for the wares of Rome and the East, but the tradesmen were gone, the marts were silent, and nothing was left but the broken jars all set in cement of cinders and ashes: the wine and the oil that once had filled them were gone with their owners.

In a bake-shop was a mill for grinding the grain, and the furnaces for baking the bread: and they say that here, in the same furnaces, the exhumers of Pompeii found nice, well baked loaves which the baker had not found time to remove from the ovens the last time he left his shop, because circumstances compelled him to leave in such a hurry.

In one house (the only building in Pompeii which no woman is now allowed to enter) were the small rooms and short beds of solid masonry, just as they were in the old times, and on the walls were pictures which looked almost as fresh as if they were painted yesterday, but which no pen could have the hardihood to describe; and here and there were Latin inscriptions – obscene scintillations of wit, scratched by hands that possibly were uplifted to Heaven for succor in the midst of a driving storm of fire before the night was done.

In one of the principal streets was a ponderous stone tank, and a water-spout that supplied it, and where the tired, heated toilers from the Campagna used to rest their right hands when they bent over to put their lips to the spout, the thick stone was worn down to a broad groove an inch or two deep. Think of the countless thousands of hands that had pressed that spot in the ages that are gone, to so reduce a stone that is as hard as iron!

They had a great public bulletin board in Pompeii – a place where announcements for gladiatorial combats, elections, and such things, were posted – not on perishable paper, but carved in enduring stone. One lady, who, I take it, was rich and well brought up, advertised a dwelling or so to rent, with baths and all the modern improvements, and several hundred shops, stipulating that the dwellings should not be put to immoral purposes. You can find out who lived in many a house in Pompeii by the carved stone door-plates affixed to them: and in the same way you can tell who they were that occupy the tombs. Everywhere around are things that reveal to you something of the customs and history of this forgotten people. But what would a volcano leave of an American city, if it once rained its cinders on it? Hardly a sign or a symbol to tell its story.

In one of these long Pompeiian halls the skeleton of a man was found, with ten pieces of gold in one hand and a large key in the other. He had seized his money and started toward the door, but the fiery tempest caught him at the very threshold, and he sank down and died. One more minute of precious time would have saved him. I saw the skeletons of a man, a woman, and two young girls. The woman had her hands spread wide apart, as if in mortal terror, and I imagined I could still trace upon her shapeless face something of the expression of wild despair that distorted it when the heavens rained fire in these streets, so many ages ago. The girls and the man lay with their faces upon their arms, as if they had tried to shield them from the enveloping cinders. In one apartment eighteen skeletons were found, all in sitting postures, and blackened places on the walls still mark their shapes and show their attitudes, like shadows. One of them, a woman, still wore upon her skeleton throat a necklace, with her name engraved upon it – *Julie Di Diomede*.

But perhaps the most poetical thing Pompeii has yielded to modern research, was that grand figure of a Roman soldier, clad in complete armor; who, true to his duty, true to his proud name of a soldier of Rome, and full of the stern courage which had given to that name its glory, stood to his post by the city gate, erect and unflinching, till the hell that raged around him *burned out* the dauntless spirit it could not conquer.

We never read of Pompeii but we think of that soldier; we cannot write of Pompeii without the natural impulse to grant to him the mention he so well deserves. Let us remember that he was a soldier – not a policeman – and so, praise him. Being a soldier, he stayed – because the warrior instinct forbade him to fly. Had he been a policeman he would have stayed, also – because he would have been asleep.

There are not half a dozen flights of stairs in Pompeii, and no other evidences that the houses were more than one story high. The people did not live in the clouds, as do the Venetians, the Genoese and Neapolitans of today.

We came out from under the solemn mysteries of this city of the Venerable Past – this city which perished, with all its old ways and its quaint old fashions about it, remote centuries ago, when the Disciples were preaching the new religion, which is as old as the hills to us now – and went dreaming among the trees that grow over acres and acres of its still buried streets and squares, till a shrill whistle and the cry of 'All aboard – last train for Naples!' woke me up and reminded me that I belonged in the nineteenth century, and was not a dusty mummy, caked with ashes and cinders, 1,800 years old. The transition was startling. The idea of a railroad train actually running to old dead Pompeii, and whistling irreverently, and calling for passengers in the most bustling and business-like way, was as strange a thing as one could imagine, and as unpoetical and disagreeable as it was strange.

Compare the cheerful life and the sunshine of this day with the horrors the younger Pliny saw here, the 9th of November, A.D. 79, when he was so bravely striving to remove his mother out of reach of harm, while she begged him, with all a mother's unselfishness, to leave her to perish and save himself.

'By this time the murky darkness had so increased that one might have believed himself abroad in a black and moonless night, or in a chamber where all the lights had been extinguished. On every hand was heard the complaints of women, the wailing of children, and the cries of men. One called his father, another his son, and another his wife, and only by their voices could they know each other. Many in their despair begged that death would come and end their distress.

'Some implored the gods to succor them, and some believed that this night was the last, the eternal night which should engulf the universe!

'Even so it seemed to me – and I consoled myself for the coming death with the reflection: *behold, the world is passing away!*'

After browsing among the stately ruins of Rome, of Baiae, of Pompeii, and after glancing down the long marble ranks of battered and nameless imperial heads that stretch down the corridors of the Vatican, one thing strikes me with a force it never had before: the unsubstantial, unlasting character of fame. Men lived long lives, in the olden time, and struggled feverishly through them, toiling like slaves, in oratory, in generalship, or in literature, and then laid them down and died, happy in the possession of an enduring history and a deathless name. Well, twenty little centuries flutter away, and what is left of these things? A crazy inscription on a block of stone, which snuffy antiquaries bother over and tangle up and make nothing out of but a bare name (which they spell wrong) – no history, no tradition, no poetry – nothing that can give it even a passing interest. What may be left of General Grant's great name forty centuries hence? This – in the Encyclopedia for A.D. 5868, possibly:

'URIAH S. (or Z.) GRAUNT – popular poet of ancient times in the Aztec provinces of the United States of British America. Some authors say flourished about A.D. 742; but the learned Ah-ah Foo-foo states that he was a contemporary of Scharkspyre, the English poet, and flourished about A.D. 1328, some three centuries after the Trojan war instead of before it. He wrote 'Rock me to Sleep, Mother.'

These thoughts sadden me. I will to bed.

Italian language

I found that a person of large intelligence could read this beautiful language with considerable facility without a dictionary, but I presently found that to such a person a grammar could be of use at times. It is because, if he does not know the weres and the wass and the maybes and the has-beenss apart, confusions and uncertainties can arise. He can get the idea that a thing is going to happen next week when the truth is that it has already happened week before last. Even more previously, sometimes. Examination and inquiry showed me that the adjectives and such things were frank and fair-minded and straightforward, and did not shuffle; it was the Verb that mixed the hands, it was the Verb that lacked stability, it was the Verb that had no permanent opinion about anything, it was the Verb that was always dodging the issue and putting out the light and making all the trouble.

Further examination, further inquiry, further reflection, confirmed this judgment, and established beyond peradventure the fact that the Verb was the storm-center. This discovery made plain the right and wise course to pursue in order to acquire certainty and exactness in understanding the statements which the newspaper was daily endeavoring to convey to me: I must catch a verb and tame it. I must find out its ways, I must spot its eccentricities, I must penetrate its disguises, I must intelligently foresee and forecast at least the commoner of the dodges it was likely to try upon a stranger in given circumstances, I must get in on its main shifts and head them off, I must learn its game and play the limit.

I had noticed, in other foreign languages, that verbs are bred in families, and that the members of each family have certain features or resemblances that are common to that family and distinguish it from the other families – the other kin, the cousins and what not.

I had noticed that this family-mark is not usually the nose or the hair, so to speak, but the tail – the Termination – and that these tails are quite definitely differentiated; insomuch that an expert can tell a pluperfect from a subjunctive by its tail as easily and as certainly as a cowboy can tell a cow from a horse by the like process, the result of observation and culture. I should explain that I am speaking of legitimate verbs, those verbs which in the slang of the grammar are called regular. There are others – I am not meaning to conceal this; others called Irregulars, born out of wedlock, of unknown and uninteresting parentage, and naturally destitute of family resemblances, as regards to all features, tails included. But of these pathetic outcasts I have nothing to say. I do not approve of them, I do not encourage them; I am prudishly delicate and sensitive, and I do not allow them to be used in my presence.

But, as I have said, I decided to catch one of the others and break it into harness. One is enough. Once familiar with its assortment of tails, you are immune; after that, no regular verb can conceal its specialty from you and make you think it is working the past or the future or the conditional or the unconditional when it is engaged in some other line of business – its tail will give it away. I found out all these things by myself, without a teacher.

I selected the verb *amare, to love*. Not for any personal reason, for I am indifferent about verbs; I care no more for one verb than for another, and have little or no respect for any of them; but in foreign languages you always begin with that one. Why, I don't know. It is merely habit, I suppose; the first teacher chose it, Adam was satisfied, and there hasn't been a successor since with originality enough to start a fresh one. For they *are* a pretty limited lot, you will admit that? Originality is not in their line; they can't think up anything new, anything to freshen up the old moss-grown dullness of the language lesson and put life and 'go' into it, and charm and grace and picturesqueness.

I knew I must look after those details myself; therefore I thought them out and wrote them down, and set for the *facchino*[v] and explained them to him, and said he must arrange a proper plant, and get together a good stock company among the *contadini*[vi], and design the costumes, and distribute the parts; and drill the troupe, and be ready in three days to begin on this verb in a shipshape and workman-like manner. I told him to put each grand division of it under a foreman, and each subdivision under a subordinate of the rank of sergeant or corporal or something like that, and to have a different uniform for each squad, so that I could tell a Pluperfect from a Compound Future without looking at the book; the whole battery to be under his own special and particular command, with the rank of Brigadier, and I to pay the freight.

I then inquired into the character and possibilities of the selected verb, and was much disturbed to find that it was over my size, it being chambered for fifty-seven rounds – fifty-seven ways of saying *I love* without reloading; and yet none of them likely to convince a girl that was laying for a title, or a title that was laying for rocks.

It seemed to me that with my inexperience it would be foolish to go into action with this *mitrailleuse*[vii], so I ordered it to the rear and told the facchino to provide something a little more primitive to start with, something less elaborate, some gentle old-fashioned flint-lock, smooth-bore, double-barreled thing, calculated to cripple at 200 yards and kill at 40 – an arrangement suitable for a beginner who could be satisfied with moderate results on the offstart and did not wish to take the whole territory in the first campaign.

But in vain. He was not able to mend the matter, all the verbs being of the same build, all Gatlings, all of the same caliber and delivery, fifty-seven to the volley, and fatal at a mile and a half. But he said the auxiliary verb *avere, to have*, was a tidy thing, and easy to handle in a seaway, and less likely to miss stays in going about than some of the others; so, upon his recommendation I chose that one, and told him to take it along and scrape its bottom and break out its spinnaker and get it ready for business.

I will explain that a facchino is a general-utility domestic. Mine was a horse-doctor in his better days, and a very good one. At the end of three days the facchino-doctor-brigadier was ready. I was also ready, with a stenographer. We were in a room called the Rope-Walk. This is a formidably long room, as is indicated by its facetious name, and is a good place for reviews. At 9:30 the F.D.B. took his place near me and gave the word of command; the drums began to rumble and thunder, the head of the forces appeared at an upper door, and the 'march-past' was on. Down they filed, a blaze of variegated color, each squad gaudy in a uniform of its own and bearing a banner inscribed with its verbal rank and quality: first the Present Tense in Mediterranean blue and old gold, then the Past Definite in scarlet and black, then the Imperfect in green and yellow, then the Indicative Future in the stars and stripes, then the Old Red Sandstone Subjunctive in purple and silver – and so on and so on, fifty-seven privates and twenty commissioned and non-commissioned officers; certainly one of the most fiery and dazzling and eloquent sights I have ever beheld. I could not keep back the tears. Presently:

'Halt!' commanded the Brigadier.
'Front–face!'
'Right dress!'
'Stand at ease!'
'One – two – three. In unison – *recite*!'

It was fine. In one noble volume of sound of all the fifty-seven Haves in the Italian language burst forth in an exalting and splendid confusion. Then came commands:

'About – face! Eyes – front! Helm alee – hard aport! Forward – march!' and the drums let go again.

When the last Termination had disappeared, the commander said the instruction drill would now begin, and asked for suggestions.

I said:

'They say *I have, thou hast, he has*, and so on, but they don't say what. It will be better, and more definite, if they have something to have; just an object, you know, a something – anything will do; anything that will give the listener a sort of personal as well as grammatical interest in their joys and complaints, you see.'

He said: 'It is a good point. Would a dog do?'

I said I did not know, but we could try a dog and see. So he sent out an aide-de-camp to give the order to add the dog.

The six privates of the Present Tense now filed in, in charge of Sergeant avere (to have), and displaying their banner. They formed in line of battle, and recited, one at a time, thus:

'*Io ho un cane*, I have a dog.'

'*Tu hai un cane*, thou hast a dog.'

'*Egli ha un cane*, he has a dog.'

'*Noi abbiamo un cane*, we have a dog.'

'*Voi avete un cane*, you have a dog.'

'*Eglino hanno un cane*, they have a dog.'

No comment followed. They returned to camp, and I reflected a while.

The commander said: 'I fear you are disappointed.'

'Yes,' I said; 'they are too monotonous, too singsong, to dead-and-alive; they have no expression, no elocution. It isn't natural; it could never happen in real life. A person who had just acquired a dog is either blame' glad or blame' sorry. He is not on the fence. I never saw a case. What the nation do you suppose is the matter with these people?'

He thought maybe the trouble was with the dog. He said:

'These are *contadini*, you know, and they have a prejudice against dogs – that is, against *marimane*. *Marimana* dogs stand guard over people's vines and olives, you know, and are very savage, and thereby a grief and an inconvenience to persons who want other people's things at night. In my judgment they have taken this dog for a *marimana*, and have soured on him.'

I saw that the dog was a mistake, and not functionable: we must try something else; something, if possible, that could evoke sentiment, interest, feeling.

'What is cat, in Italian?' I asked.

'Gatto.'

'Is it a gentleman cat, or a lady?'

'Gentleman cat.'

'How are these people as regards that animal?'

'We-ll, they – they –'

'You hesitate: that is enough. How are they about chickens?'

He tilted his eyes toward heaven in mute ecstasy. I understood.

'What is chicken, in Italian?' I asked.

'Pollo, *podere*.' (Podere is Italian for master. It is a title of courtesy, and conveys reverence and admiration.) 'Pollo is one chicken by itself; when there are enough present to constitute a plural, it is *polli*.'

'Very well, *polli* will do. Which squad is detailed for duty next?'

'The Past Definite.'

'Send out and order it to the front – with chickens. And let them understand that we don't want any more of this cold indifference.'

He gave the order to an aide, adding, with a haunting tenderness in his tone and a watering mouth in his aspect:

'Convey to them the conception that these are unprotected chickens.'

He turned to me, saluting with his hand to his temple, and explained, 'It will inflame their interest in the poultry, sire.'

A few minutes elapsed. Then the squad marched in and formed up, their faces glowing with enthusiasm, and the file-leader shouted:

'*Ebbi polli*, I had chickens!'

'Good!' I said. 'Go on, the next.'

'*Avest polli*, thou hadst chickens!"

'Fine! Next!'

'*Ebbe polli*, he had chickens!'

'*Moltimoltissimo*! Go on, the next!'

'*Avemmo polli*, we had chickens!'

'*Basta-basta aspettatto Avanti* – last man – *charge*!

'*Ebbero polli*, they had chickens!'

Then they formed in echelon, by columns of fours, refused the left, and retired in great style on the double-quick. I was enchanted, and said:

'Now, doctor, that is something *like*! Chickens are the ticket, there is no doubt about it. What is the next squad?'

'The Imperfect.'

'How does it go?'

'*Io avena*, I had, *Tu avevi*, thou hadst, *Egli avena*, he had, *Noi av –*'

'Wait – we've just *had* the Hads. What are you giving me?'

'But this is another breed.'

'What do we want of another breed? Isn't one breed enough? *Had* is *had*, and your tricking it out in a fresh way of spelling isn't going to make it any hadder than it was before; now you know that yourself.'

'But there is a distinction – they are not just the same Hads.'

'How do you make it out?'

'Well, you use that first Had when you are referring to something that happened at a named and sharp and perfectly definite moment; you use the other when the thing happened at a vaguely defined time and in a more prolonged and indefinitely continuous way.'

'Why, doctor, it is pure nonsense; you know it yourself. Look here: if I have had a had, or have wanted to have had a had, or was in a position right then and there to have had a had that hadn't had any chance to go out hadding on account of this foolish discrimination which lets one Had go hadding in any kind of indefinite grammatical weather but restricts the other one to definite and datable meteoric convulsions, and keeps it pining around and watching the barometer all the time, and liable to get sick through confinement and lack of exercise, and all that sort of thing, why — why, the inhumanity of it is enough, let alone the wanton superfluity and uselessness of any such a loafing consumptive hospital-bird of a Had taking up room and cumbering the place for nothing. These finical refinements revolt me; it is not right, it is not honorable; it is constructive nepotism to keep in office a Had that is so delicate it can't come out when the wind's in the nor'west – I won't have this dude on the payroll. Cancel his exequator; and look here –'

'But you miss the point. It is like this. You see –'

'Never mind explaining, I don't care anything about it. Six Hads is enough for me; anybody that needs twelve, let him subscribe; I don't want any stock in a Had Trust. Knock out the Prolonged and Indefinitely Continuous; four-fifths of it is water, anyway.'

'But I beg you, *podere*! It is often quite indispensable in cases where –'

'Pipe the next squad to the assault!'

But it was not to be; for at that moment the dull boom of the noon gun floated up out of far-off Florence, followed by the usual softened jangle of churchbells, Florentine and suburban, that bursts out in murmurous response; by labor-union law the *colazione*[viii] must stop; stop promptly, stop instantly, stop definitely, like the chosen and best of the breed of Hads.

Spain

We were approaching the famed Pillars of Hercules, and already the African one, 'Ape's Hill', a grand old mountain with summit streaked with granite ledges, was in sight. The other, the great Rock of Gibraltar, was yet to come. The ancients considered the Pillars of Hercules the head of navigation and the end of the world. The information the ancients didn't have was very voluminous. Even the prophets wrote book after book and epistle after epistle, yet never once hinted at the existence of a great continent on our side of the water; yet they must have known it was there, I should think.

In a few moments a lonely and enormous mass of rock, standing seemingly in the center of the wide strait and apparently washed on all sides by the sea, swung magnificently into view, and we needed no tedious traveled parrot to tell us it was Gibraltar. There could not be two rocks like that in one kingdom.

The Rock of Gibraltar is about a mile and a half long, I should say, by 1,400 to 1,500 feet high, and a quarter of a mile wide at its base. One side and one end of it come about as straight up out of the sea as the side of a house, the other end is irregular and the other side is a steep slant which an army would find very difficult to climb. At the foot of this slant is the walled town of Gibraltar – or rather the town occupies part of the slant. Everywhere – on hillside, in the precipice, by the sea, on the heights – everywhere you choose to look, Gibraltar is clad with masonry and bristling with guns. It makes a striking and lively picture from whatsoever point you contemplate it. It is pushed out into the sea on the end of a flat, narrow strip of land, and is suggestive of a 'gob' of mud on the end of a shingle. A few hundred yards of this flat ground at its base belongs to the English, and then, extending across the strip from the Atlantic to the Mediterranean, a distance of a quarter of a mile, comes the 'Neutral Ground', a space 200 or 300 yards wide, which is free to both parties.

'Are you going through Spain to Paris?' That question was bandied about the ship day and night from Fayal to Gibraltar, and I thought I never could get so tired of hearing any one combination of words again or more tired of answering, 'I don't know.' At the last moment six or seven had sufficient decision of character to make up their minds to go, and did go, and I felt a sense of relief at once – it was forever too late now and I could make up my mind at my leisure not to go. I must have a prodigious quantity of mind; it takes me as much as a week sometimes to make it up.

But behold how annoyances repeat themselves. We had no sooner gotten rid of the Spain distress than the Gibraltar guides started another – a tiresome repetition of a legend that had nothing very astonishing about it, even in the first place: 'That high hill yonder is called the Queen's Chair; it is because one of the queens of Spain placed her chair there when the French and Spanish troops were besieging Gibraltar, and said she would never move from the spot till the English flag was lowered from the fortresses. If the English hadn't been gallant enough to lower the flag for a few hours one day, she'd have had to break her oath or die up there.'

We rode on asses and mules up the steep, narrow streets and entered the subterranean galleries the English have blasted out in the rock. These galleries are like spacious railway tunnels, and at short intervals in them great guns frown out upon sea and town through portholes 500 or 600 feet above the ocean. There is a mile or so of this subterranean work, and it must have cost a vast deal of money and labor. The gallery guns command the peninsula and the harbors of both oceans, but they might as well not be there, I should think, for an army could hardly climb the perpendicular wall of the rock anyhow. Those lofty portholes afford superb views of the sea, though. At one place, where a jutting crag was hollowed out into a great chamber whose furniture was huge cannon and whose windows were portholes, a glimpse was caught of a hill not far away, and a soldier said:

'That high hill yonder is called the Queen's Chair; it is because a queen of Spain placed her chair there once when the French and Spanish troops were besieging Gibraltar, and said she would never move from the spot till the English flag was lowered from the fortresses. If the English hadn't been gallant enough to lower the flag for a few hours one day, she'd have had to break her oath or die up there.'

On the topmost pinnacle of Gibraltar we halted a good while, and no doubt the mules were tired. They had a right to be. The military road was good, but rather steep, and there was a good deal of it. The view from the narrow ledge was magnificent; from it vessels seeming like the tiniest little toy boats were turned into noble ships by the telescopes, and other vessels that were fifty miles away and even sixty, they said, and invisible to the naked eye, could be clearly distinguished through those same telescopes. Below, on one side, we looked down upon an endless mass of batteries and on the other straight down to the sea.

While I was resting ever so comfortably on a rampart, and cooling my baking head in the delicious breeze, an officious guide belonging to another party came up and said:

'Senor, that high hill yonder is called the Queen's Chair –'

'Sir, I am a helpless orphan in a foreign land. Have pity on me. Don't – now *don't* inflict that most in-*fernal* old legend on me anymore today!'

There – I had used strong language after promising I would never do so again; but the provocation was more than human nature could bear. If you had been bored so, when you had the noble panorama of Spain and Africa and the blue Mediterranean spread abroad at your feet, and wanted to gaze and enjoy and surfeit yourself in its beauty in silence, you might have even burst into stronger language than I did.

Gibraltar has stood several protracted sieges, one of them of nearly four years' duration (it failed), and the English only captured it by stratagem. The wonder is that anybody should ever dream of trying so impossible a project as the taking it by assault – and yet it has been tried more than once.

The Moors held the place 1,200 years ago, and a staunch old castle of theirs of that date still frowns from the middle of the town, with moss-grown battlements and sides well scarred by shots fired in battles and sieges that are forgotten now. A secret chamber in the rock behind it was discovered some time ago, which contained a sword of exquisite workmanship, and some quaint old armor of a fashion that antiquaries are not acquainted with, though it is supposed to be Roman. Roman armor and Roman relics of various kinds have been found in a cave in the sea extremity of Gibraltar; history says Rome held this part of the country about the Christian era, and these things seem to confirm the statement.

In that cave also are found human bones, crusted with a very thick, stony coating, and wise men have ventured to say that those men not only lived before the flood, but as much as 10,000 years before it. It may be true – it looks reasonable enough – but as long as those parties can't vote anymore, the matter can be of no great public interest. In this cave likewise are found skeletons and fossils of animals that exist in every part of Africa, yet within memory and tradition have never existed in any portion of Spain save this lone peak of Gibraltar! So the theory is that the channel between Gibraltar and Africa was once dry land, and that the low, neutral neck between Gibraltar and the Spanish hills behind it was once ocean, and of course that these African animals, being over at Gibraltar (after rock, perhaps – there is plenty there), got closed out when the great change occurred. The hills in Africa, across the channel, are full of apes, and there are now and always have been apes on the rock of Gibraltar – but not elsewhere in Spain! The subject is an interesting one.

There is an English garrison at Gibraltar of 6,000 or 7,000 men, and so uniforms of flaming red are plenty; and red and blue, and undress costumes of snowy white, and also the queer uniform of the bare-kneed Highlander; and one sees soft-eyed

Spanish girls from San Roque, and veiled Moorish beauties (I suppose they are beauties) from Tarifa, and turbaned, sashed, and trousered Moorish merchants from Fez, and long-robed, bare-legged, ragged Muhammadan vagabonds from Tetuan and Tangier, some brown, some yellow and some as black as virgin ink – and Jews from all around, in gabardine, skullcap, and slippers, just as they are in pictures and theaters, and just as they were 3,000 years ago, no doubt. You can easily understand that a tribe (somehow our pilgrims suggest that expression, because they march in a straggling procession through these foreign places with such an Indian-like air of complacency and independence about them) like ours, made up from fifteen or sixteen states of the Union, found enough to stare at in this shifting panorama of fashion today.

Every now and then my glove purchase in Gibraltar last night intrudes itself upon me. Dan and the ship's surgeon and I had been up to the great square, listening to the music of the fine military bands and contemplating English and Spanish female loveliness and fashion, and at nine o'clock were on our way to the theater, when we met the General, the Judge, the Commodore, the Colonel, and the Commissioner of the United States of America to Europe, Asia, and Africa, who had been to the Club House to register their several titles and impoverish the bill of fare; and they told us to go over to the little variety store near the Hall of Justice and buy some kid gloves. They said they were elegant and very moderate in price. It seemed a stylish thing to go to the theater in kid gloves, and we acted upon the hint. A very handsome young lady in the store offered me a pair of blue gloves. I did not want blue, but she said they would look very pretty on a hand like mine. The remark touched me tenderly. I glanced furtively at my hand, and somehow it did seem rather a comely member. I tried a glove on my left and blushed a little. Manifestly the size was too small for me. But I felt gratified when she said:

'Oh, it is just right!' Yet I knew it was no such thing.

I tugged at it diligently, but it was discouraging work. She said: 'Ah! I see *you* are accustomed to wearing kid gloves – but some gentlemen are so awkward about putting them on.'

It was the last compliment I had expected. I only understand putting on the buckskin article perfectly. I made another effort and tore the glove from the base of the thumb into the palm of the hand – and tried to hide the rent. She kept up her compliments, and I kept up my determination to deserve them or die:

'Ah, you have had experience! [A rip down the back of the hand.] They are just right for you – your hand is very small – if they tear you need not pay for them. [A rent across the middle.] I can always tell when a gentleman understands putting on kid gloves. There is a grace about it that only comes with long practice.' The whole after-guard of the glove 'fetched away', as the sailors say, the fabric parted across the knuckles, and nothing was left but a melancholy ruin.

I was too much flattered to make an exposure and throw the merchandise on the angel's hands. I was hot, vexed, confused, but still happy; but I hated the other boys for taking such an absorbing interest in the proceedings. I wished they were in Jericho. I felt exquisitely mean when I said cheerfully:

'This one does very well; it fits elegantly. I like a glove that fits. No, never mind, ma'am, never mind; I'll put the other on in the street. It is warm here.'

It *was* warm. It was the warmest place I ever was in. I paid the bill, and as I passed out with a fascinating bow I thought I detected a light in the woman's eye that was gently ironical; and when I looked back from the street, and she was laughing all to herself about something or other, I said to myself with withering sarcasm, 'Oh, certainly; *you* know how to put on kid gloves, don't you? A self-complacent ass, ready to be flattered out of your senses by every petticoat that chooses to take the trouble to do it!'

The silence of the boys annoyed me. Finally Dan said musingly:

'Some gentlemen don't know how to put on kid gloves at all, but some do.'

And the doctor said (to the moon, I thought):

'But it is always easy to tell when a gentleman is used to putting on kid gloves.'

Dan soliloquized after a pause:

'Ah, yes; there is a grace about it that only comes with long, very long practice.'

'Yes, indeed, I've noticed that when a man hauls on a kid glove like he was dragging a cat out of an ash hole by the tail, *he* understands putting on kid gloves; *he's* had ex– '

'Boys, enough of a thing's enough! You think you are very smart, I suppose, but I don't. And if you go and tell any of those old gossips in the ship about this thing, I'll never forgive you for it; that's all.'

They let me alone then for the time being. We always let each other alone in time to prevent ill feeling from spoiling a joke. But they had bought gloves, too, as I did. We threw all the purchases away together this morning. They were coarse, unsubstantial, freckled all over with broad yellow splotches, and could neither stand wear nor public exhibition. We had entertained an angel unawares, but we did not take her in. She did that for us.

Greece

We spent one pleasant day skirting along the Isles of Greece. They are very mountainous. Their prevailing tints are gray and brown, approaching to red. Little white villages surrounded by trees, nestle in the valleys or roost upon the lofty perpendicular sea-walls.

We had one fine sunset – a rich carmine flush that suffused the western sky and cast a ruddy glow far over the sea. Fine sunsets seem to be rare in this part of the world – or at least, striking ones. They are soft, sensuous, lovely – they are exquisite refined, effeminate, but we have seen no sunsets here yet like the gorgeous conflagrations that flame in the track of the sinking sun in our high northern latitudes.

But what were sunsets to us, with the wild excitement upon us of approaching the most renowned of cities! What cared we for outward visions, when Agamemnon, Achilles, and a thousand other heroes of the great Past were marching in ghostly procession through our fancies? What were sunsets to us, who were about to live and breathe and walk in actual Athens; yea, and go far down into the dead centuries and bid in person for the slaves, Diogenes and Plato, in the public marketplace, or gossip with the neighbors about the siege of Troy or the splendid deeds of Marathon? We scorned to consider sunsets.

We arrived, and entered the ancient harbor of the Piraeus at last. We dropped anchor within half a mile of the village. Away off, across the undulating Plain of Attica, could be seen a little square-topped hill with a something on it, which our glasses soon discovered to be the ruined edifices of the citadel of the Athenians, and most prominent among them loomed the venerable Parthenon. So exquisitely clear and pure is this wonderful atmosphere that every column of the noble structure was discernible through the telescope, and even the smaller ruins about it assumed some semblance of shape. This at a distance of five or six miles. In the valley, near the Acropolis (the square-topped hill before spoken of), Athens itself could be vaguely made out with an ordinary lorgnette. Everybody was anxious to get ashore and visit these classic localities as quickly as possible. No land we had yet seen had aroused such universal interest among the passengers.

But bad news came. The commandant of the Piraeus came in his boat, and said we must either depart or else get outside the harbor and remain imprisoned in our ship, under rigid quarantine, for eleven days! So we took up the anchor and moved outside, to lie a dozen hours or so, taking in supplies, and then sail for Constantinople. It was the bitterest disappointment we had yet experienced. To lie a whole day in sight of the Acropolis, and yet be obliged to go away without visiting Athens! Disappointment was hardly a strong enough word to describe the circumstances.

All hands were on deck, all the afternoon, with books and maps and glasses, trying to determine which 'narrow rocky ridge' was the Areopagus, which sloping hill the Pnyx, which elevation the Museum Hill, and so on. And we got things confused. Discussion became heated, and party spirit ran high. Church members were gazing with emotion upon a hill which they said was the one St Paul preached from, and another faction claimed that that hill was Hymettus, and another that it was Pentelicon! After all the trouble, we could be certain of only one thing – the square-topped hill was the Acropolis, and the grand ruin that crowned it was the Parthenon, whose picture we knew in infancy in the school books.

We inquired of everybody who came near the ship, whether there were guards in the Piraeus, whether they were strict, what the chances were of capture should any of us slip ashore, and in case any of us made the venture and were caught, what would be probably done to us? The answers were discouraging: there was a strong guard or police force; the Piraeus was a small town, and any stranger seen in it would surely attract attention – capture would be certain. The commandant said the punishment would be 'heavy'; when asked 'how heavy?' he said it would be 'very severe' – that was all we could get out of him.

At eleven o'clock at night, when most of the ship's company were abed, four of us stole softly ashore in a small boat, a clouded moon favoring the enterprise, and started two and two, and far apart, over a low hill, intending to go clear around the Piraeus, out of the range of its police. Picking our way so stealthily over that rocky, nettle-grown eminence, made me feel a good deal as if I were on my way somewhere to steal something. My immediate comrade and I talked in an undertone about quarantine laws and their penalties, but we found nothing cheering in the subject. I was posted. Only a few days before, I was talking with our captain, and he mentioned the case of a man who swam ashore from a quarantined ship somewhere, and got imprisoned six months for it; and when he was in Genoa a few years ago, a captain of a quarantined ship went in his boat to a departing ship, which was already outside of the harbor, and put a letter on board to be taken to his family, and the authorities imprisoned him three months for it, and then conducted him and his ship fairly to sea, and warned him never to show himself in that port again while he lived. This kind of conversation did no good, further than to give a sort of dismal interest to our quarantine-breaking expedition, and so we dropped it. We made the entire circuit of the town without seeing anybody but one man, who stared at us curiously, but said nothing, and a dozen persons asleep on the ground before their doors, whom we walked among and never woke – but we woke up dogs enough, in all conscience – we always had one or two barking at our heels, and several times we had as many as ten and twelve at once. They made such a preposterous din that persons aboard our ship said they could tell how we were progressing for a long time, and where we were, by the barking of the dogs. The clouded moon still favored us. When we had made the whole circuit, and were passing among the houses on the further side of the town, the moon came out splendidly, but we no longer feared the light. As we approached a well, near a house, to get a drink, the owner merely glanced at us and went within. He left the quiet, slumbering town at our mercy. I record it here proudly, that we didn't do anything to it.

Seeing no road, we took a tall hill to the left of the distant Acropolis for a mark, and steered straight for it over all obstructions, and over a little rougher piece of country than exists anywhere else outside of the State of Nevada, perhaps. Part of the way it was covered with small, loose stones – we trod on six at a time, and they all rolled. Another part of it was dry, loose, newly-ploughed ground. Still another part of it was a long stretch of low grapevines, which were tanglesome and troublesome, and which we took to be brambles. The Attic Plain, barring the grapevines, was a barren, desolate, unpoetical waste – I wonder what it was in Greece's Age of Glory, 500 years before Christ?

In the neighborhood of one o'clock in the morning, when we were heated with fast walking and parched with thirst, Denny exclaimed, 'Why, these weeds are grapevines!' and in five minutes we had a score of bunches of large, white, delicious grapes, and were reaching down for more when a dark shape rose mysteriously up out of the shadows beside us and said 'Ho!' And so we left.

In ten minutes more we struck into a beautiful road, and unlike some others we had stumbled upon at intervals, it led in the right direction. We followed it. It was broad, and smooth, and white – handsome and in perfect repair, and shaded on both sides for a mile or so with single ranks of trees, and also with luxuriant vineyards. Twice we entered and stole grapes, and the second time somebody shouted at us from some invisible place. Whereupon we left again. We speculated in grapes no more on that side of Athens.

Shortly we came upon an ancient stone aqueduct, built upon arches, and from that time forth we had ruins all about us – we were approaching our journey's end. We could not see the Acropolis now or the high hill, either, and I wanted to follow the road till we were abreast of them, but the others overruled me, and we toiled laboriously up the stony hill immediately in our front – and from its summit saw another – climbed it and saw another! It was an hour of exhausting work. Soon we came upon a row of open graves, cut in the solid rock – (for a while one of them served Socrates for a prison) – we passed around the shoulder of the hill, and the citadel, in all its ruined magnificence, burst upon us! We hurried across the ravine and up a winding road, and stood on the old Acropolis, with the prodigious walls of the citadel towering above our heads. We did not stop to inspect their massive blocks of marble, or measure their height, or guess at their extraordinary thickness, but passed at once through a great arched passage like a railway tunnel, and went straight to the gate that leads to the ancient temples. It was locked! So, after all, it seemed that we were not to see the great Parthenon face to face. We sat down and held a council of war. Result: the gate was only a flimsy structure of wood – we would break it down. It seemed like desecration, but then we had traveled far, and our necessities were urgent. We could not hunt up guides and keepers – we must be on the ship before daylight. So we argued. This was all very fine, but when we came to break the gate, we could not do it. We moved around an angle of the wall and found a low bastion – eight feet high without – ten or twelve within. Denny prepared to scale it, and we got ready to follow. By dint of hard scrambling he finally straddled the top, but some loose stones crumbled away and fell with a crash into the court within. There was instantly a banging of doors and a shout. Denny dropped from the wall in a twinkling, and we retreated in disorder to the gate. Xerxes took that mighty citadel 480 years before Christ, when his five millions of soldiers and camp-followers followed him to Greece, and if we four Americans could have remained unmolested five minutes longer, we would have taken it too.

The garrison had turned out – four Greeks. We clamored at the gate, and they admitted us. [Bribery and corruption.]

We crossed a large court, entered a great door, and stood upon a pavement of purest white marble, deeply worn by footprints. Before us, in the flooding moonlight, rose the noblest ruins we had ever looked upon – the Propylae; a small Temple of Minerva;

the Temple of Hercules, and the grand Parthenon. [We got these names from the Greek guide, who didn't seem to know more than seven men ought to know.] These edifices were all built of the whitest Pentelic marble, but have a pinkish stain upon them now. Where any part is broken, however, the fracture looks like fine loaf sugar. Six caryatides, or marble women, clad in flowing robes, support the portico of the Temple of Hercules, but the porticos and colonnades of the other structures are formed of massive Doric and Ionic pillars, whose flutings and capitals are still measurably perfect, notwithstanding the centuries that have gone over them and the sieges they have suffered. The Parthenon, originally, was 226 feet long, 100 wide, and 70 high, and had two rows of great columns, eight in each, at either end, and single rows of seventeen each down the sides, and was one of the most graceful and beautiful edifices ever erected.

Most of the Parthenon's imposing columns are still standing, but the roof is gone. It was a perfect building 250 years ago, when a shell dropped into the Venetian magazine stored here, and the explosion which followed wrecked and unroofed it. I remember but little about the Parthenon, and I have put in one or two facts and figures for the use of other people with short memories. Got them from the guidebook.

As we wandered thoughtfully down the marble-paved length of this stately temple, the scene about us was strangely impressive. Here and there, in lavish profusion, were gleaming white statues of men and women, propped against blocks of marble, some of them armless, some without legs, others headless – but all looking mournful in the moonlight, and startlingly human! They rose up and confronted the midnight intruder on every side – they stared at him with stony eyes from unlooked-for nooks and recesses; they peered at him over fragmentary heaps far down the desolate corridors; they barred his way in the midst of the broad forum, and solemnly pointed with handless arms the way from the sacred fane; and through the roofless temple the moon looked down, and banded the floor and darkened the scattered fragments and broken statues with the slanting shadows of the columns.

What a world of ruined sculpture was about us! Set up in rows – stacked up in piles – scattered broadcast over the wide area of the Acropolis – were hundreds of crippled statues of all sizes and of the most exquisite workmanship; and vast fragments of marble that once belonged to the entablatures, covered with bas-reliefs representing battles and sieges, ships of war with three and four tiers of oars, pageants and processions – everything one could think of. History says that the temples of the Acropolis were filled with the noblest works of Praxiteles and Phidias, and of many a great master in sculpture besides – and surely these elegant fragments attest it.

We walked out into the grass-grown, fragment-strewn court beyond the Parthenon. It startled us, every now and then, to see a stony white face stare suddenly up at us out of the grass with its dead eyes. The place seemed alive with ghosts. I half expected to see the Athenian heroes of twenty centuries ago glide out of the shadows and steal into the old temple they knew so well and regarded with such boundless pride.

The full moon was riding high in the cloudless heavens, now. We sauntered carelessly and unthinkingly to the edge of the lofty battlements of the citadel, and looked down – a vision! And such a vision! Athens by moonlight! The prophet that thought the splendors of the New Jerusalem were revealed to him, surely saw this instead! It lay in the level plain right under our feet – all spread abroad like a picture – and we looked down upon it as we might have looked from a balloon. We saw no semblance of a street, but every house, every window, every clinging vine, every projection was as distinct and sharply marked as if the time were noonday; and yet there was no glare, no glitter, nothing harsh or repulsive – the noiseless city was flooded with the mellowest light that ever streamed from the moon, and seemed like some living creature wrapped in peaceful slumber. On its further side was a little temple, whose delicate pillars and ornate front glowed with a rich lustre that chained the eye like a spell; and nearer by, the palace of the king reared its creamy walls out of the midst of a great garden of shrubbery that was flecked all over with a random shower of amber lights – a spray of golden sparks that lost their brightness in the glory of the moon, and glinted softly upon the sea of dark foliage like the pallid stars of the milky-way. Overhead the stately columns, majestic still in their ruin – underfoot the dreaming city – in the distance the silver sea – not on the broad earth is there another picture half so beautiful!

As we turned and moved again through the temple, I wished that the illustrious men who had sat in it in the remote ages could visit it again and reveal themselves to our curious eyes – Plato, Aristotle, Demosthenes, Socrates, Phocion, Pythagoras, Euclid, Pindar, Xenophon, Herodotus, Praxiteles and Phidias, Zeuxis the painter. What a constellation of celebrated names! But more than all, I wished that old Diogenes, groping so patiently with his lantern, searching so zealously for one solitary honest man in all the world, might meander along and stumble on our party. I ought not to say it, may be, but still I suppose he would have put out his light.

It occurred to us, after a while, that if we wanted to get home before daylight betrayed us, we had better be moving. So we hurried away. When far on our road, we had a parting view of the Parthenon, with the moonlight streaming through its open colonnades and touching its capitals with silver. As it looked then, solemn, grand, and beautiful it will always remain in our memories.

As we marched along, we began to get over our fears, and ceased to care much about quarantine scouts or anybody else. We grew bold and reckless; and once, in a sudden burst of courage, I even threw a stone at a dog. It was a pleasant reflection, though, that I did not hit him, because his master might just possibly have been a policeman. Inspired by this happy failure, my valor became utterly uncontrollable, and at intervals I absolutely whistled, though on a moderate key. But boldness breeds boldness, and shortly I plunged into a vineyard, in the full light of the moon, and captured a gallon of superb grapes, not even minding the presence of a peasant who rode by on a mule. Denny and Birch followed my example.

Now I had grapes enough for a dozen, but then Jackson was all swollen up with courage, too, and he was obliged to enter a vineyard presently. The first bunch he seized brought trouble. A frowsy, bearded brigand advancing with celerity. The brigand shouted again, but still we advanced. It was getting late, and we had no time to fool away on every ass that wanted to drivel Greek platitudes to us. We would just as soon have talked with him as not if we had not been in a hurry. Presently Denny said, 'Those fellows are following us!'

We turned, and, sure enough, there they were – three fantastic pirates armed with guns. We slackened our pace to let them come up, and in the meantime I got out my cargo of grapes and dropped them firmly but reluctantly into the shadows by the wayside. But I was not afraid. I only felt that it was not right to steal grapes. And all the more so when the owner was around – and not only around, but with his friends around also. The villains came up and searched a bundle Dr Birch had in his hand, and scowled upon him when they found it had nothing in it but some holy rocks from Mars Hill, and these were not contraband. They evidently suspected him of playing some wretched fraud upon them, and seemed half inclined to scalp the party. But finally they dismissed us with a warning, couched in excellent Greek, I suppose, and dropped tranquilly in our wake. When they had gone 300 yards they stopped, and we went on rejoiced. But behold, another armed rascal came out of the shadows and took their place, and followed us 200 yards. Then he delivered us over to another miscreant, who emerged from some mysterious place, and he in turn to another! For a mile and a half our rear was guarded all the while by armed men. I never traveled in so much state before in all my life.

It was a good while after that before we ventured to steal any more grapes, and when we did we stirred up another troublesome brigand, and then we ceased all further speculation in that line. I suppose that fellow that rode by on the mule posted all the sentinels, from Athens to the Piraeus, about us.

Every field on that long route was watched by an armed sentinel, some of whom had fallen asleep, no doubt, but were on hand, nevertheless. This shows what sort of a country modern Attica is – a community of questionable characters. These men were not there to guard their possessions against strangers, but against each other; for strangers seldom visit Athens and the Piraeus, and when they do, they go in daylight, and can buy all the grapes they want for a trifle. The modern inhabitants are confiscators and falsifiers of high repute, if gossip speaks truly concerning them, and I freely believe it does.

Just as the earliest tinges of the dawn flushed the eastern sky and turned the pillared Parthenon to a broken harp hung in the pearly horizon, we closed our thirteenth mile of weary, round-about marching, and emerged upon the seashore abreast the ships, with our usual escort of 1,500 Piraean dogs howling at our heels. We hailed a boat that was 200 or 300 yards from shore, and discovered in a moment that it was a police-boat on the lookout for any quarantine-breakers that might chance to be abroad. So we dodged – we were used to that by this time – and when the scouts reached the spot we had so lately occupied, we were absent. They cruised along the shore, but in the wrong direction, and shortly our own boat issued from the gloom and took us aboard. They had heard our signal on the ship. We rowed noiselessly away, and before the police-boat came in sight again, we were safe at home once more.

Four more of our passengers were anxious to visit Athens, and started half an hour after we returned; but they had not been ashore five minutes till the police discovered and chased them so hotly that they barely escaped to their boat again, and that was all. They pursued the enterprise no further.

Two other passengers ran the blockade successfully last night. So we learned this morning. They slipped away so quietly that they were not missed from the ship for several hours. They had the hardihood to march into the Piraeus in the early dusk and hire a carriage. They ran some danger of adding two or three months' imprisonment to the other novelties of their Holy Land Pleasure Excursion. I admire 'cheek'. But they went and came safely, and never walked a step.

Germany

Next morning brought good news – our trunks had arrived from Hamburg at last. Let this be a warning to the reader. The Germans are very conscientious, and this trait makes them very particular. Therefore if you tell a German you want a thing done immediately, he takes you at your word; he thinks you mean what you say; so he does that thing immediately – according to his idea of immediately – which is about a week; that is, it is a week if it refers to the building of a garment, or it is an hour and a half if it refers to the cooking of a trout. Very well; if you tell a German to send your trunk to you by 'slow freight', he takes you at your word; he sends it by 'slow freight', and you cannot imagine how long you will go on enlarging your admiration of the expressiveness of that phrase in the German tongue, before you get that trunk. The hair on my trunk was soft and thick and youthful, when I got it ready for shipment in Hamburg; it was baldheaded when it reached Heidelberg. However, it was still sound, that was a comfort, it was not battered in the least; the baggagemen seemed to be conscientiously careful, in Germany, of the baggage entrusted to their hands. There was nothing now in the way of our departure, therefore we set about our preparations.

Naturally my chief solicitude was about my collection of Ceramics. Of course I could not take it with me, that would be inconvenient, and dangerous besides. I took advice, but the best brick-a-brackers were divided as to the wisest course to pursue; some said pack the collection and warehouse it; others said try to get it into the Grand Ducal Museum at Mannheim for safe keeping. So I divided the collection, and followed the advice of both parties. I set aside, for the Museum, those articles which were the most frail and precious.

Among these was my Etruscan tear-jug. I have made a little sketch of it here; that thing creeping up the side is not a bug, it is a hole. I bought this tear-jug of a dealer in antiquities for 450 dollars. It is very rare. The man said the Etruscans used to keep tears or something in these things, and that it was very hard to get hold of a broken one, now.

I also set aside my Henri II plate. See sketch from my pencil; it is in the main correct, though I think I have foreshortened one end of it a little too much, perhaps. This is very fine and rare; the shape is exceedingly beautiful and unusual. It has wonderful decorations on it, but I am not able to reproduce them. It cost more than the tear-jug, as the dealer said there was not another plate just like it in the world. He said there was much false Henri II ware around, but that the genuineness of this piece was unquestionable.

He showed me its pedigree, or its history, if you please; it was a document which traced this plate's movements all the way down from its birth – showed who bought it, from whom, and what he paid for it – from the first buyer down to me, whereby I saw that it had gone steadily up from 35 cents to 700 dollars. He said that the whole Ceramic world would be informed that it was now in my possession and would make a note of it, with the price paid.

There were Masters in those days, but, alas – it is not so now. Of course the main preciousness of this piece lies in its color; it is that old sensuous, pervading, ramifying, interpolating, transboreal blue which is the despair of modern art. The little sketch which I have made of this gem cannot and does not do it justice, since I have been obliged to leave out the color. But I've got the expression, though.

However, I must not be frittering away the reader's time with these details. I did not intend to go into any detail at all, at first, but it is the failing of the true ceramiker, or the true devotee in any department of brick-a-brackery, that once he gets his tongue or his pen started on his darling theme, he cannot well stop until he drops from exhaustion. He has no more sense of the flight of time than has any other lover when talking of his sweetheart. The very 'marks' on the bottom of a piece of rare crockery are able to throw me into a gibbering ecstasy; and I could forsake a drowning relative to help dispute about whether the stopple of a departed Buon Retiro scent-bottle was genuine or spurious.

Many people say that for a male person, bric-a-brac hunting is about as robust a business as making doll-clothes, or decorating Japanese pots with decalcomania butterflies would be, and these people fling mud at the elegant Englishman, Byng, who wrote a book called 'The Bric-A-Brac Hunter', and make fun of him for chasing around after what they choose to call 'his despicable trifles'; and for 'gushing' over these trifles; and for exhibiting his 'deep infantile delight' in what they call his 'tuppenny collection of beggarly trivialities'; and for beginning his book with a picture of himself seated, in a 'sappy, self-complacent attitude, in the midst of his poor little ridiculous bric-a-brac junk shop'.

It is easy to say these things; it is easy to revile us, easy to despise us; therefore, let these people rail on; they cannot feel as Byng and I feel – it is their loss, not ours. For my part I am content to be a brick-a-bracker and a ceramiker – more, I am proud to be so named. I am proud to know that I lose my reason as immediately in the presence of a rare jug with an illustrious mark on the bottom of it, as if I had just emptied that jug. Very well; I packed and stored a part of my collection, and the rest of it I placed in the care of the Grand Ducal Museum in Mannheim, by permission. My Old Blue China Cat remains there yet. I presented it to that excellent institution.

I had but one misfortune with my things. An egg which I had kept back from breakfast that morning, was broken in packing. It was a great pity. I had shown it to the best connoisseurs in Heidelberg, and they all said it was an antique. We spent a day or two in farewell visits, and then left for Baden-Baden. We had a pleasant trip to it, for the Rhine valley is always lovely. The only trouble was that the trip was too short. If I remember rightly it only occupied a couple of hours, therefore I judge that the distance was very little, if any, over fifty miles. We quitted the train at Oos, and walked the entire remaining distance to Baden-Baden, with the exception of a lift of less than an hour which we got on a passing wagon, the weather being exhaustingly warm. We came into town on foot.

One of the first persons we encountered, as we walked up the street, was the Rev. Mr —, an old friend from America – a lucky encounter, indeed, for his is a most gentle, refined, and sensitive nature, and his company and companionship are a genuine refreshment. We knew he had been in Europe some time, but were not at all expecting to run across him. Both parties burst forth into loving enthusiasms, and Rev. Mr — said: 'I have got a brimful reservoir of talk to pour out on you, and an empty one ready and thirsting to receive what you have got; we will sit up till midnight and have a good satisfying interchange, for I leave here early in the morning.' We agreed to that, of course.

I had been vaguely conscious, for a while, of a person who was walking in the street abreast of us; I had glanced furtively at him once or twice, and noticed that he was a fine, large, vigorous young fellow, with an open, independent countenance, faintly shaded with a pale and even almost imperceptible crop of early down, and that he was clothed from head to heel in cool and enviable snow-white linen. I thought I had also noticed that his head had a sort of listening tilt to it. Now about this time the Rev. Mr — said:

'The sidewalk is hardly wide enough for three, so I will walk behind; but keep the talk going, keep the talk going, there's no time to lose, and you may be sure I will do my share.' He ranged himself behind us, and straightway that stately snow-white young fellow closed up to the sidewalk alongside him, fetched him a cordial slap on the shoulder with his broad palm, and sung out with a hearty cheeriness:

'*Americans* for two-and-a-half and the money up! Hey?'

The Reverend winced, but said mildly:

'Yes – we are Americans.'

'Lord love you, you can just bet that's what – I – am, every time! Put it there!'

He held out his Sahara of his palm, and the Reverend laid his diminutive hand in it, and got so cordial a shake that we heard his glove burst under it.

'Say, didn't I put you up right?'

'Oh, yes.'

'Sho! I spotted you for *my* kind the minute I heard your clack. You been over here long?'

'About four months. Have you been over long?'

'*Long*? Well, I should say so! Going on two years, by geeminy! Say, are you homesick?'

'No, I can't say that I am. Are you?'

'Oh, *hell*, yes!' This with immense enthusiasm.

The Reverend shrunk a little, in his clothes, and we were aware, rather by instinct than otherwise, that he was throwing out signals of distress to us; but we did not interfere or try to succor him, for we were quite happy.

The young fellow hooked his arm into the Reverend's, now, with the confiding and grateful air of a waif who has been longing for a friend, and a sympathetic ear, and a chance to lisp once more the sweet accents of the mother-tongue – and then he limbered up the muscles of his mouth and turned himself loose – and with such a relish! Some of his words were not Sunday-school words, so I am obliged to put blanks where they occur.

'Yes indeedy! If – I – *ain't* an American there ain't any Americans, that's all. And when I heard you fellows gassing away in the good old American language, I'm – if it wasn't all I could do to keep from hugging you! My tongue's all warped with trying to curl it around these – forsaken wind-galled nine-jointed German words here; now I *tell* you it's awful good to lay it over a Christian word once more and kind of let the old taste soak it. I'm from western New York. My name is Cholley Adams. I'm a student, you know. Been here going on two years. I'm learning to be a horse-doctor! I *like* that part of it, you know, but – these people, they won't learn a fellow in his own language, they make him learn in German; so before I could tackle the horse-doctoring I had to tackle this miserable language.

'First off, I thought it would certainly give me the botts, but I don't mind now. I've got it where the hair's short, I think; and dontchuknow, they made me learn Latin, too. Now between you and me, I wouldn't give a – for all the Latin that was ever jabbered; and the first thing – I – calculate to do when I get through, is to just sit down and forget it. 'Twon't take me long, and I don't mind the time, anyway. And I tell you what! the difference between school-teaching over yonder and school-teaching over here – sho! *We* don't know anything about it! Here you've got to peg and peg and peg and there just ain't any let-up – and what you learn here, you've got to know, dontchuknow – or else you'll have one of these – spavined, spectacles, ring-boned, knock-kneed old professors in your hair. I've been here long *enough*, and I'm getting blessed tired of it, mind I *tell* you. The old man wrote me that he was coming over in June, and said he'd take me home in August, whether I was done with my education or not, but durn him, he didn't come; never said why; just sent me a hamper of Sunday-school books, and told me to be good, and hold on a while. I don't take to Sunday-school books, dontchuknow – I don't hanker after them when I can get pie – but I *read* them, anyway, because whatever the old man tells me to *do*, that's the thing that I'm a-going to do, or tear something, you know. I buckled in and read all those books, because he wanted me to; but that kind of thing don't excite *me*, I like something *hearty*. But I'm awful homesick. I'm homesick from ear-socket to crupper, and from crupper to hock-joint; but it ain't any use, I've got to stay here, till the old man drops the rag and give the word – yes, *sir*, right here in this – country I've got to linger till the old man says *come*! – and you bet your bottom dollar, Johnny, it *ain't* just as easy as it is for a cat to have twins!'

At the end of this profane and cordial explosion he fetched a prodigious '*Whoosh*!' to relieve his lungs and make recognition of the heat, and then he straightway dived into his narrative again for 'Johnny's' benefit, beginning, 'Well, – it ain't any use talking, some of those old American words *do* have a kind of a bully swing to them; a man can *express* himself with 'em – a man can get at what he wants to *say*, dontchuknow.'

When we reached our hotel and it seemed that he was about to lose the Reverend, he showed so much sorrow, and begged so hard and so earnestly that the Reverend's heart was not hard enough to hold out against the pleadings – so he went away with the parent-honoring student, like a right Christian, and took supper with him in his lodgings, and sat in the surf-beat of his slang and profanity till near midnight, and then left him – left him pretty well talked out, but grateful 'clear down to his frogs', as he expressed it. The Reverend said it had transpired during the interview that 'Cholley' Adams's father was an extensive dealer in horses in western New York; this accounted for Cholley's choice of a profession. The Reverend brought away a pretty high opinion of Cholley as a manly young fellow, with stuff in him for a useful citizen; he considered him rather a rough gem, but a gem, nevertheless.

❧

Sunday is the great day on the continent – the free day, the happy day. One can break the Sabbath in a hundred ways without committing any sin.

We do not work on Sunday, because the commandment forbids it; the Germans do not work on Sunday, because the commandment forbids it. We rest on Sunday, because the commandment requires it; the Germans rest on Sunday because the commandment requires it. But in the definition of the word 'rest' lies all the difference. With us, its Sunday meaning is, stay in the house and keep still; with the Germans its Sunday and week-day meanings seem to be the same – rest the *tired part*, and never mind the other parts of the frame; rest the tired part, and use the means best calculated to rest that particular part. Thus: If one's duties have kept him in the house all the week, it will rest him to be out on Sunday; if his duties have required him to read weighty and serious matter all the week, it will rest him to read light matter on Sunday; if his occupation has busied him with death and funerals all the week, it will rest him to go to the theater Sunday night and put in two or three hours laughing at a comedy; if he is tired with digging ditches or felling trees all the week, it will rest him to lie quiet in the house on Sunday; if the hand, the arm, the brain, the tongue, or any other member, is fatigued with inanition, it is not to be rested by adding a day's inanition; but if a member is fatigued with exertion, inanition is the right rest for it. Such is the way in which the Germans seem to define the word 'rest'; that is to say, they rest a member by recreating, recuperating, restoring its forces. But our definition is less broad. We all rest alike on Sunday – by secluding ourselves and keeping still, whether that is the surest way to rest the most of us or not. The Germans make the actors, the preachers, etc., work on Sunday. We encourage the preachers, the editors, the printers, etc., to work on Sunday, and imagine that none of the sin of it falls upon us; but I do not know how we are going to get around the fact that if it is wrong for the printer to work at his trade on Sunday it must be equally wrong for the preacher to work at his, since the commandment has made no exception in his favor. We buy Monday morning's paper and read it, and thus encourage Sunday printing. But I shall never do it again.

The Germans remember the Sabbath-day to keep it holy, by abstaining from work, as commanded; we keep it holy by abstaining from work, as commanded, and by also abstaining from play, which is not commanded. Perhaps we constructively *break* the command to rest, because the resting we do is in most cases only a name, and not a fact.

These reasonings have sufficed, in a measure, to mend the rent in my conscience which I made by traveling to Baden-Baden that Sunday. We arrived in time to furbish up and get to the English church before services began. We arrived in considerable style, too, for the landlord had ordered the first carriage that could be found, since there was no time to lose, and our coachman was so splendidly liveried that we were probably mistaken for a brace of stray dukes; why else were we honored with a pew all to ourselves, away up among the very elect at the left of the chancel? That was my first thought. In the pew directly in front of us sat an elderly lady, plainly and cheaply dressed; at her side sat a young lady with a very sweet face, and she also was quite simply dressed; but around us and about us were clothes and jewels which it would do anybody's heart good to worship in.

I thought it was pretty manifest that the elderly lady was embarrassed at finding herself in such a conspicuous place arrayed in such cheap apparel; I began to feel sorry for her and troubled about her. She tried to seem very busy with her prayer-book and her responses, and unconscious that she was out of place, but I said to myself, 'She is not succeeding – there is a distressed tremulousness in her voice which betrays increasing embarrassment.' Presently the Savior's name was mentioned, and in her flurry she lost her head completely, and rose and courtesied, instead of making a slight nod as everybody else did. The sympathetic blood surged to my temples and I turned and gave those fine birds what I intended to be a beseeching look, but my feelings got the better of me and changed it into a look which said, 'If any of you pets of fortune laugh at this poor soul, you will deserve to be flayed for it.' Things went from bad to worse, and I shortly found myself mentally taking the unfriended lady under my protection. My mind was wholly upon her. I forgot all about the sermon. Her embarrassment took stronger and stronger hold upon her; she got to snapping the lid of her smelling-bottle – it made a loud, sharp sound, but in her trouble she snapped and snapped away, unconscious of what she was doing. The last extremity was reached when the collection-plate began its rounds; the moderate people threw in pennies, the nobles and the rich contributed silver, but she laid a twenty-mark gold piece upon the book-rest before her with a sounding slap! I said to myself, 'She has parted with all her little hoard to buy the consideration of these unpitying people – it is a sorrowful spectacle.' I did not venture to look around this time; but as the service closed, I said to myself, 'Let them laugh, it is their opportunity; but at the door of this church they shall see her step into our fine carriage with us, and our gaudy coachman shall drive her home.'

Then she rose – and all the congregation stood while she walked down the aisle. She was the Empress of Germany!

No – she had not been so much embarrassed as I had supposed. My imagination had got started on the wrong scent, and that is always hopeless; one is sure, then, to go straight on misinterpreting everything, clear through to the end. The young lady with her imperial Majesty was a maid of honor – and I had been taking her for one of her boarders, all the time.

This is the only time I have ever had an Empress under my personal protection; and considering my inexperience, I wonder I got through with it so well. I should have been a little embarrassed myself if I had known earlier what sort of a contract I had on my hands.

We found that the Empress had been in Baden-Baden several days. It is said that she never attends any but the English form of church service.

I lay abed and read and rested from my journey's fatigues the remainder of that Sunday, but I sent my agent to represent me at the afternoon service, for I never allow anything to interfere with my habit of attending church twice every Sunday.

There was a vast crowd in the public grounds that night to hear the band play the 'Fremersberg'. This piece tells one of the old legends of the region; how a great noble of the Middle Ages got lost in the mountains, and wandered about with his dogs in a violent storm, until at last the faint tones of a monastery bell, calling the monks to a midnight service, caught his ear, and he followed the direction the sounds came from and was saved. A beautiful air ran through the music, without ceasing, sometimes loud and strong, sometimes so soft that it could hardly be distinguished – but it was always there; it swung grandly along through the shrill whistling of the storm-wind, the rattling patter of the rain, and the boom and crash of the thunder; it wound soft and low through the lesser sounds, the distant ones, such as the throbbing of the convent bell, the melodious winding of the hunter's horn, the distressed bayings of his dogs, and the solemn chanting of the monks; it rose again, with a jubilant ring, and mingled itself with the country songs and dances of the peasants assembled in the convent hall to cheer up the rescued huntsman while he ate his supper. The instruments imitated all these sounds with a marvelous exactness. More than one man started to raise his umbrella when the storm burst forth and the sheets of mimic rain came driving by; it was hardly possible to keep from putting your hand to your hat when the fierce wind began to rage and shriek; and it was not possible to refrain from starting when those sudden and charmingly real thunder-crashes were let loose.

I suppose the 'Fremersberg' is a very low-grade music; I know, indeed, that it *must* be low-grade music, because it delighted me, warmed me, moved me, stirred me, uplifted me, enraptured me, that I was full of cry all the time, and mad with enthusiasm. My soul had never had such a scouring out since I was born. The solemn and majestic chanting of the monks was not done by instruments, but by men's voices; and it rose and fell, and rose again in that rich confusion of warring sounds, and pulsing bells, and the stately swing of that ever-present enchanting air, and it seemed to me that nothing but the very lowest of low-grade music could be so divinely beautiful. The great crowd which the 'Fremersberg' had called out was another evidence that it was low-grade music; for only the few are educated up to a point where high-grade music gives pleasure. I have never heard enough classic music to be able to enjoy it. I dislike the opera because I want to love it and can't.

I suppose there are two kinds of music – one kind which one feels, just as an oyster might, and another sort which requires a higher faculty, a faculty which must be assisted and developed by teaching. Yet if base music gives certain of us wings, why should we want any other? But we do. We want it because the higher and better like it. We want it without giving it the necessary time and trouble; so we climb into that upper tier, that dress-circle, by a lie; we *pretend* we like it. I know several of that sort of people – and I propose to be one of them myself when I get home with my fine European education.

And then there is painting. What a red rag is to a bull, Turner's 'Slave Ship' was to me, before I studied art. Mr Ruskin is educated in art up to a point where that picture throws him into as mad an ecstasy of pleasure as it used to throw me into one of rage, last year, when I was ignorant. His cultivation enables him – and me, now – to see water in that glaring yellow mud, and natural effects in those lurid explosions of mixed smoke and flame, and crimson sunset glories; it reconciles him – and me, now – to the floating of iron cable-chains and other unfloatable things; it reconciles us to fishes swimming around on top of the mud – I mean the water. The most of the picture is a manifest impossibility – that is to say, a lie; and only rigid cultivation can enable a man to find truth in a lie. But it enabled Mr Ruskin to do it, and it has enabled me to do it, and I am thankful for it. A Boston newspaper reporter went and took a look at the Slave Ship floundering about in that fierce conflagration of reds and yellows, and said it reminded him of a tortoise-shell cat having a fit in a platter of tomatoes. In my then uneducated state, that went home to my non-cultivation, and I thought here is a man with an unobstructed eye. Mr Ruskin would have said: this person is an ass. That is what I would say, now.

However, our business in Baden-Baden this time, was to join our courier. I had thought it best to hire one, as we should be in Italy, by and by, and we did not know the language. Neither did he. We found him at the hotel, ready to take charge of us. I asked him if he was 'all fixed'. He said he was. That was very true. He had a trunk, two small satchels, and an umbrella. I was to pay him fifty-five dollars a month and railway fares. On the continent the railway fare on a trunk is about the same as it is on a man. Couriers do not have to pay any board and lodging. This seems a great saving to the tourist – at first. It does not occur to the tourist that somebody pays that man's board and lodging. It occurs to him by and by, however, in one of his lucid moments.

German language

I went often to look at the collection of curiosities in Heidelberg Castle, and one day I surprised the keeper of it with my German. I spoke entirely in that language. He was greatly interested; and after I had talked a while he said my German was very rare, possibly a 'unique'; and wanted to add it to his museum.

If he had known what it had cost me to acquire my art, he would also have known that it would break any collector to buy it. Harris and I had been hard at work on our German during several weeks at that time, and although we had made good progress, it had been accomplished under great difficulty and annoyance, for three of our teachers had died in the meantime. A person who has not studied German can form no idea of what a perplexing language it is.

Surely there is not another language that is so slipshod and systemless, and so slippery and elusive to the grasp. One is washed about in it, hither and thither, in the most helpless way; and when at last he thinks he has captured a rule which offers firm ground to take a rest on amid the general rage and turmoil of the ten parts of speech, he turns over the page and reads, 'Let the pupil make careful note of the following *exceptions*.' He runs his eye down and finds that there are more exceptions to the rule than instances of it. So overboard he goes again, to hunt for another Ararat and find another quicksand. Such has been, and continues to be, my experience. Every time I think I have got one of these four confusing 'cases' where I am master of it, a seemingly insignificant preposition intrudes itself into my sentence, clothed with an awful and unsuspected power, and crumbles the ground from under me. For instance, my book inquires after a certain bird – (it is always inquiring after things which are of no sort of consequence to anybody): 'Where is the bird?' Now the answer to this question – according to the book – is that the bird is waiting in the blacksmith shop on account of the rain. Of course no bird would do that, but then you must stick to the book. Very well, I begin to cipher out the German for that answer. I begin at the wrong end, necessarily, for that is the German idea. I say to myself, 'Regen (rain) is masculine – or maybe it is feminine – or possibly neuter – it is too much trouble to look now. Therefore, it is either *der* (the) Regen, or *die* (the) Regen, or *das* (the) Regen, according to which gender it may turn out to be when I look. In the interest of science, I will cipher it out on the hypothesis that it is masculine. Very well – then *the* rain is *der* Regen, if it is simply in the quiescent state of being *mentioned*, without enlargement or discussion – nominative case; but if this rain is lying around, in a kind of a general way on the ground, it is then definitely located, it is *doing something* – that is, *resting* (which is one of the German grammar's ideas of doing something), and this throws the rain into the dative case, and makes it *dem* Regen. However, this rain is not resting, but is doing something *actively*, – it is falling – to interfere with the bird, likely – and this indicates *movement*, which has the effect of sliding it into the accusative case and changing *dem* Regen into *den* Regen.' Having completed the grammatical horoscope of this matter, I answer up confidently and state in German that the bird is staying in the blacksmith shop 'wegen (on account of) *den* Regen.' Then the teacher lets me softly down with the remark that whenever the word 'wegen' drops into a sentence, it *always* throws that subject into the *genitive* case, regardless of consequences – and therefore this bird stayed in the blacksmith shop 'wegen *des* Regens'.

N.B. – I was informed, later, by a higher authority, that there was an 'exception' which permits one to say 'wegen *den* Regen' in certain peculiar and complex circumstances, but that this exception is not extended to anything but rain.

There are ten parts of speech, and they are all troublesome. An average sentence, in a German newspaper, is a sublime and impressive curiosity; it occupies a quarter of a column; it contains all the ten parts of speech – not in regular order, but mixed; it is built mainly of compound words constructed by the writer on the spot, and not to be found in any dictionary – six or seven words compacted into one, without joint or seam – that is, without hyphens; it treats of fourteen or fifteen different subjects, each enclosed in a parenthesis of its own, with here and there extra parentheses, making pens within pens: finally, all the parentheses and reparentheses are massed together between a couple of king-parentheses, one of which is placed in the first line of the majestic sentence and the other in the middle of the last line of it – *after which comes the verb*, and you find out for the first time what the man has been talking about; and after the verb – merely by way of ornament, as far as I can make out – the writer shovels in '*haben sind gewesen gehabt haven geworden sein*', or words to that effect, and the monument is finished. I suppose that this closing hurrah is in the nature of the flourish to a man's signature – not necessary, but pretty. German books are easy enough to read when you hold them before the looking-glass or stand on your head – so as to reverse the construction – but I think that to learn to read and understand a German newspaper is a thing which must always remain an impossibility to a foreigner.

Yet even the German books are not entirely free from attacks of the Parenthesis distemper – though they are usually so mild as to cover only a few lines, and therefore when you at last get down to the verb it carries some meaning to your mind because you are able to remember a good deal of what has gone before. Now here is a sentence from a popular and excellent German novel – with a slight parenthesis in it. I will make a perfectly literal translation, and throw in the parenthesis-marks and some hyphens for the assistance of the reader – though in the original there are no parenthesis-marks or hyphens, and the reader is left to flounder through to the remote verb the best way he can:

> But when he, upon the street, the (in-satin-and-silk-covered-now-very-unconstrained-after-the-newest-fashioned-dressed) government counselor's wife met, etc., etc.
>
> *Wenn er aber auf der Strasse der in Sammt und Seide gehuellten jetz sehr ungenirt nach der neusten mode gekleideten Regierungsräthin begegnet.*

That is from 'The Old Mamselle's Secret', by Mrs Marlitt. And that sentence is constructed upon the most approved German model. You observe how far that verb is from the reader's base of operations; well, in a German newspaper they put their verb away over on the next page; and I have heard that sometimes after stringing along the exciting preliminaries and parentheses for a column or two, they get in a hurry and have to go to press without getting to the verb at all. Of course, then, the reader is left in a very exhausted and ignorant state.

We have the Parenthesis disease in our literature, too; and one may see cases of it every day in our books and newspapers: but with us it is the mark and sign of an unpracticed writer or a cloudy intellect, whereas with the Germans it is doubtless the mark and sign of a practiced pen and of the presence of that sort of luminous intellectual fog which stands for clearness among these people. For surely it is not clearness – it necessarily can't be clearness. Even a jury would have penetration enough to discover that. A writer's ideas must be a good deal confused, a good deal out of line and sequence, when he starts out to say that a man met a counselor's wife in the street, and then right in the midst of this so simple undertaking halts these approaching people and makes them stand still until he jots down an inventory of the woman's dress. That is manifestly absurd. It reminds a person of those dentists who secure your instant and breathless interest in a tooth by taking a grip on it with the forceps, and then stand there and drawl through a tedious anecdote before they give the dreaded jerk. Parentheses in literature and dentistry are in bad taste.

The Germans have another kind of parenthesis, which they make by splitting a verb in two and putting half of it at the beginning of an exciting chapter and the *other half* at the end of it. Can anyone conceive of anything more confusing than that? These things are called 'separable verbs'. The German grammar is blistered all over with separable verbs; and the wider the two portions of one of them are spread apart, the better the author of the crime is pleased with his performance. A favorite one is *reiste ab* – which means departed. Here is an example which I culled from a novel and reduced to English:

The trunks being now ready, he *de-* after kissing his mother and sisters, and once more pressing to his bosom his adored Gretchen, who, dressed in simple white muslin, with a single tuberose in the ample folds of her rich brown hair, had tottered feebly down the stairs, still pale from the terror and excitement of the past evening, but longing to lay her poor aching head yet once again upon the breast of him whom she loved more dearly than life itself, *parted*.

However, it is not well to dwell too much on the separable verbs. One is sure to lose his temper early; and if he sticks to the subject, and will not be warned, it will at last either soften his brain or petrify it. Personal pronouns and adjectives are a fruitful nuisance in this language, and should have been left out. For instance, the same sound, *sie*, means *you*, and *it* means *she*, and *it* means *her*, and *it* means *it*, and *it* means *they*, and *it* means *them*. Think of the ragged poverty of a language which has to make one word do the work of six – and a poor little weak thing of only three letters at that. But mainly, think of the exasperation of never knowing which of these meanings the speaker is trying to convey. This explains why, whenever a person says *sie* to me, I generally try to kill him, if a stranger.

Now observe the adjective. Here was a case where simplicity would have been an advantage; therefore, for no other reason, the inventor of this language complicated it all he could. When we wish to speak of our 'good friend or friends', in our enlightened tongue, we stick to the one form and have no trouble or hard feeling about it; but with the German tongue it is different. When a German gets his hands on an adjective, he declines it, and keeps on declining it until the common sense is all declined out of it. It is as bad as Latin. He says, for instance:

SINGULAR

Nominative – Mein gut*er* Freund, my good friend. Genitive – Mein*es* Gut*en* Freund*es*, of my good friend. Dative – Mein*em* gut*en*

Freund, to my good friend. Accusative – Mein*en* gut*en* Freund, my good friend.

PLURAL

Nominative – Mein*e* gut*en* Freund*e*, my good friends. Genitive – Mein*er* gut*en* Freund*e*, of my good friends. Dative – Mein*en* gut*en* Freund*en*, to my good friends. Accusative – Mein*e* gut*en* Freund*e*, my good friends.

Now let the candidate for the asylum try to memorize those variations, and see how soon he will be elected. One might better go without friends in Germany than take all this trouble about them. I have shown what a bother it is to decline a good (male) friend; well this is only a third of the work, for there is a variety of new distortions of the adjective to be learned when the object is feminine, and still another when the object is neuter. Now there are more adjectives in this language than there are black cats in Switzerland, and they must all be as elaborately declined as the examples above suggested. Difficult?– troublesome? – these words cannot describe it. I heard a Californian student in Heidelberg say, in one of his calmest moods, that he would rather decline two drinks than one German adjective.

The inventor of the language seems to have taken pleasure in complicating it in every way he could think of. For instance, if one is casually referring to a house, *Haus*, or a horse, *Pferd*, or a dog, *Hund*, he spells these words as I have indicated; but if he is referring to them in the Dative case, he sticks on a foolish and unnecessary e and spells them *Hause*, *Pferde*, *Hunde*. So, as an added *e* often signifies the plural, as the s does with us, the new student is likely to go on for a month making twins out of a dative dog before he discovers his mistake; and on the other hand, many a new student who could ill afford loss, has bought and paid for two dogs and only got one of them, because he ignorantly bought that dog in the dative singular when he really supposed he was talking plural – which left the law on the seller's side, of course, by the strict rules of grammar, and therefore a suit for recovery could not lie.

In German, all the nouns begin with a capital letter. Now that is a good idea; and a good idea, in this language, is necessarily conspicuous from its lonesomeness. I consider this capitalizing of nouns a good idea, because by reason of it you are almost always able to tell a noun the minute you see it. You fall into error occasionally, because you mistake the name of a person for the name of a thing, and waste a good deal of time trying to dig a meaning out of it. German names almost always do mean something, and this helps to deceive the student. I translated a passage one day, which said that 'the infuriated tigress broke loose and utterly ate up the unfortunate fir forest' (Tannenwald). When I was girding up my loins to doubt this, I found out that Tannenwald in this instance was a man's name.

Every noun has a gender, and there is no sense or system in the distribution; so the gender of each must be learned separately and by heart. There is no other way. To do this one has to have a memory like a memorandum book. In German, a young lady has no sex, while a turnip has. Think what overwrought reverence that shows for the turnip, and what callous disrespect for the girl. See how it looks in print – I translate this from a conversation in one of the best of the German Sunday-school books:

> Gretchen. 'Wilhelm, where is the turnip?'
> Wilhelm. 'She has gone to the kitchen.'

> Gretchen. 'Where is the accomplished and beautiful English maiden?'
> Wilhelm. 'It has gone to the opera.'

To continue with the German genders: a tree is male, its buds are female, its leaves are neuter; horses are sexless, dogs are male, cats are female – tomcats included, of course; a person's mouth, neck, bosom, elbows, fingers, nails, feet, and body are of the male sex, and his head is male or neuter according to the word selected to signify it, and *not* according to the sex of the individual who wears it – for in Germany all the women wear either male heads or sexless ones; a person's nose, lips, shoulders, breast, hands, and toes are of the female sex; and his hair, ears, eyes, chin, legs, knees, heart, and conscience haven't any sex at all. The inventor of the language probably got what he knew about a conscience from hearsay.

Now, by the above dissection, the reader will see that in Germany a man may *think* he is a man, but when he comes to look into the matter closely, he is bound to have his doubts; he finds that in sober truth he is a most ridiculous mixture; and if he ends by trying to comfort himself with the thought that he can at least depend on a third of this mess as being manly and masculine, the humiliating second thought will quickly remind him that in this respect he is no better off than any woman or cow in the land.

In German it is true that by some oversight of the inventor of the language, a woman is a female; but a wife (*Weib*) is not – which is unfortunate. A Wife, here, has no sex; she is neuter; so, according to the grammar, a fish is *he*, his scales are *she*, but a fishwife is neither. To describe a wife as sexless may be called under-description; that is bad enough, but over-description is surely worse. A German speaks of an Englishman as the *engländer*; to change the sex, he adds inn, and that stands for Englishwoman – *engländerinn*. That seems descriptive enough, but still it is not exact enough for a German; so he precedes the word with that article which indicates that the creature to follow is feminine, and writes it down thus: 'die Engländerinn', – which means 'the she-Englishwoman'. I consider that that person is over-described.

Well, after the student has learned the sex of a great number of nouns, he is still in a difficulty, because he finds it impossible to persuade his tongue to refer to things as 'he' and 'she', and 'him' and 'her', which it has been always accustomed to refer to as 'it'. When he even frames a German sentence in his mind, with the hims and hers in the right places, and then works up his courage to the utterance-point, it is no use – the moment he begins to speak his tongue flies the track and all those labored males and females come out as 'its'. And even when he is reading German to himself, he always calls those things 'it', whereas he ought to read in this way:

Tale of The Fishwife and Its Sad Fate

(I capitalize the nouns, in the German (and ancient English) fashion.)

It is a bleak Day. Hear the Rain, how he pours, and the Hail, how he rattles; and see the Snow, how he drifts along, and of the Mud, how deep he is! Ah the poor Fishwife, it is stuck fast in the Mire; it has dropped its Basket of Fishes; and its Hands have been cut by the Scales as it seized some of the falling Creatures; and one Scale has even got into its Eye, and it cannot get her out. It opens its Mouth to cry for Help; but if any Sound comes out of him, alas he is drowned by the raging of the Storm. And now a Tomcat has got one of the Fishes and she will surely escape with him. No, she bites off a Fin, she holds her in her Mouth – will she swallow her? No, the Fishwife's brave Mother-dog deserts his Puppies and rescues the Fin – which he eats, himself, as his Reward. O, horror, the Lightning has struck the Fish-basket; he sets him on Fire; see the Flame, how she licks the doomed Utensil with her red and angry Tongue; now she attacks the helpless Fishwife's Foot – she burns him up, all but the big Toe, and even *she* is partly consumed; and still she spreads, still she waves her fiery Tongues; she attacks the Fishwife's Leg and destroys *it*; she attacks its Hand and destroys *her* also; she attacks the Fishwife's Leg and destroys *her* also; she attacks its Body and consumes *him*; she wreathes herself about its Heart and *it* is consumed; next about its Breast, and in a Moment *she* is a Cinder; now she reaches its Neck – He goes; now its Chin – *it* goes; now its Nose – *she* goes. In another Moment, except Help come, the Fishwife will be no more. Time presses – is there none to succor and save? Yes! Joy, joy, with flying Feet the she-Englishwoman comes! But alas, the generous she-Female is too late: where now is the fated Fishwife? It has ceased from its Sufferings, it has gone to a better Land; all that is left of it for its loved Ones to lament over, is this poor smoldering Ash-heap. Ah, woeful, woeful Ash-heap! Let us take him up tenderly, reverently, upon the lowly Shovel, and bear him to his long Rest, with the Prayer that when he rises again it will be a Realm where he will have one good square responsible Sex, and have it all to himself, instead of having a mangy lot of assorted Sexes scattered all over him in Spots.

There, now, the reader can see for himself that this pronoun business is a very awkward thing for the unaccustomed tongue. I suppose that in all languages the similarities of look and sound between words which have no similarity in meaning are a fruitful source of perplexity to the foreigner. It is so in our tongue, and it is notably the case in the German. Now there is that troublesome word *vermählt*: to me it has so close a resemblance – either real or fancied – to three or four other words, that I never know whether it means despised, painted, suspected or married; until I look in the dictionary, and then I find it means the latter. There are lots of such words and they are a great torment. To increase the difficulty there are words which *seem* to resemble each other, and yet do not; but they make just as much trouble as if they did. For instance, there is the word *vermiethen* (to let, to lease, to hire); and the word *verheirathen* (another way of saying to marry). I heard of an Englishman who knocked at a man's door in Heidelberg and proposed, in the best German he could command, to 'verheirathen' that house. Then there are some words which mean one thing when you emphasize the first syllable, but mean something very different if you throw the emphasis on the last syllable. For instance, there is a word which means a runaway, or the act of glancing through a book, according to the placing of the emphasis; and another word which signifies to associate with a man, or to avoid him, according to where you put the emphasis – and you can generally depend on putting it in the wrong place and getting into trouble.

There are some exceedingly useful words in this language. *Schlag*, for example; and *Zug*. There are three-quarters of a column of *Schlags* in the dictionary, and a column and a half of Zugs. The word *Schlag* means blow, stroke, dash, hit, shock, clap, slap, time, bar, coin, stamp, kind, sort, manner, way, apoplexy, wood-cutting, enclosure, field, forest-clearing. This is its simple and *exact* meaning – that is to say, its restricted, its fettered meaning; but there are ways by which you can set it free, so that it can soar away, as on the wings of the morning, and never be at rest. You can hang any word you please to its tail, and make it mean anything you want to. You can begin with *Schlag-ader*, which means artery, and you can hang on the whole dictionary, word by word, clear through the alphabet to *Schlag-Wasser*, which means bilge-water – and including *Schlag-Mutter*, which means mother-in-law.

Just the same with *Zug*. Strictly speaking, *Zug* means pull, tug, draught, procession, march, progress, flight, direction, expedition, train, caravan, passage, stroke, touch, line, flourish, trait of character, feature, lineament, chess-move, organ-stop, team, whiff, bias, drawer, propensity, inhalation, disposition: but that thing which it does not mean – when all its legitimate pennants have been hung on, has not been discovered yet.

One cannot overestimate the usefulness of *Schlag* and *Zug*. Armed just with these two, and the word *also*, what cannot the foreigner on German soil accomplish? The German word *also* is the equivalent of the English phrase 'You know', and does not mean anything at all – in *talk*, though it sometimes does in print. Every time a German opens his mouth an *also* falls out; and every time he shuts it he bites one in two that was trying to get out.

Now, the foreigner, equipped with these three noble words, is master of the situation. Let him talk right along, fearlessly; let him pour his indifferent German forth, and when he lacks for a word, let him heave a *Schlag* into the vacuum; all the chances are that it fits it like a plug, but if it doesn't let him promptly heave a *Zug* after it; the two together can hardly fail to bung the hole; but if, by a miracle, they *should* fail, let him simply say *also*!

and this will give him a moment's chance to think of the needful word. In Germany, when you load your conversational gun it is always best to throw in a *Schlag* or two and a *Zug* or two, because it doesn't make any difference how much the rest of the charge may scatter, you are bound to bag something with *them*. Then you blandly say *also*, and load up again. Nothing gives such an air of grace and elegance and unconstraint to a German or an English conversation as to scatter it full of 'Alsos' or 'You knows'.

In my notebook I find this entry:

> July 1. – In the hospital yesterday, a word of thirteen syllables was successfully removed from a patient – a North German from near Hamburg; but as most unfortunately the surgeons had opened him in the wrong place, under the impression that he contained a panorama, he died. The sad event has cast a gloom over the whole community.

That paragraph furnishes a text for a few remarks about one of the most curious and notable features of my subject – the length of German words. Some German words are so long that they have a perspective. Observe these examples:

Freundschaftsbezeigungen.
Dilettantenaufdringlichkeiten.
Stadtverordnetenversammlungen.

These things are not words, they are alphabetical processions. And they are not rare; one can open a German newspaper at any time and see them marching majestically across the page – and if he has any imagination he can see the banners and hear the music, too. They impart a martial thrill to the meekest subject. I take a great interest in these curiosities. Whenever I come across a good one, I stuff it and put it in my museum. In this way I have made quite a valuable collection. When I get duplicates, I exchange with other collectors, and thus increase the variety of my stock. Here are some specimens which I lately bought at an auction sale of the effects of a bankrupt bric-a-brac hunter:

Generalstaatsverordnetenversammlungen.
Alterthumswissenschaften.
Kinderbewahrungsanstalten.
Unabhängigkeitserklärungen.
Wiedererstellungbestrebungen.
Waffenstillstandsunterhandlungen.

Of course when one of these grand mountain ranges goes stretching across the printed page, it adorns and ennobles that literary landscape – but at the same time it is a great distress to the new student, for it blocks up his way; he cannot crawl under it, or climb over it, or tunnel through it. So he resorts to the dictionary for help, but there is no help there. The dictionary must draw the line somewhere – so it leaves this sort of words out. And it is right, because these long things are hardly legitimate words, but are rather combinations of words, and the inventor of them ought to have been killed. They are compound words with the hyphens left out. The various words used in building them are in the dictionary, but in a very scattered condition; so you can hunt the materials out, one by one, and get at the meaning at last, but it is a tedious and harassing business. I have tried this process upon some of the above examples. 'Freundshaftsbezeigungen' seems to be 'Friendship demonstrations', which is only a foolish and clumsy way of saying 'demonstrations of friendship'. 'Unabhängigkeitserklärungen' seems to be 'Independencedeclarations', which is no improvement upon 'Declarations of Independence', so far as I can see. 'Generalstaatsverordnetenversammlungen' seems to be 'General-statesrepresentativesmeetings', as nearly as I can get at it – a mere rhythmical, gushy euphemism for 'meetings of the legislature', I judge. We used to have a good deal of this sort of crime in our literature, but it has gone out now. We used to speak of a thing as a 'never-to-be-forgotten' circumstance, instead of cramping it into the simple and sufficient word 'memorable' and then going calmly about our business as if nothing had happened. In those days we were not content to embalm the thing and bury it decently, we wanted to build a monument over it.

But in our newspapers the compounding-disease lingers a little to the present day, but with the hyphens left out, in the German fashion. This is the shape it takes: instead of saying 'Mr Simmons, clerk of the county and district courts, was in town yesterday', the new form puts it thus: 'Clerk of the County and District Courts Simmons was in town yesterday.' This saves neither time nor ink, and has an awkward sound besides. One often sees a remark like this in our papers: 'Mrs Assistant District Attorney Johnson returned to her city residence yesterday for the season.' That is a case of really unjustifiable compounding; because it not only saves no time or trouble, but confers a title on Mrs Johnson which she has no right to. But these little instances are trifles indeed, contrasted with the ponderous and dismal German system of piling jumbled compounds together. I wish to submit the following local item, from a Mannheim journal, by way of illustration:

> In the daybeforeyesterdayshortlyaftereleveno'clock Night, the inthistownstandingtavern called 'The Wagoner' was downburnt. When the fire to the onthedownburninghouseresting Stork's Nest reached, flew the parent Storks away. But when the bythenraging, firesurrounded Nest itself caught Fire, straightway plunged the quickreturning Mother-Stork into the Flames and died, her Wings over her young ones outspread.

Even the cumbersome German construction is not able to take the pathos out of that picture – indeed, it somehow seems to strengthen it. This item is dated away back yonder months ago. I could have used it sooner, but I was waiting to hear from the Father-stork. I am still waiting.

'*Also!*' If I had not shown that the German is a difficult language, I have at least intended to do so. I have heard of an American student who was asked how he was getting along with his German, and who answered promptly: 'I am not getting along at all. I have worked at it hard for three level months, and all

I have got to show for it is one solitary German phrase – "Zwei Glas" (two glasses of beer).' He paused for a moment, reflectively; then added with feeling: 'But I've got that *solid*!'

And if I have not also shown that German is a harassing and infuriating study, my execution has been at fault, and not my intent. I heard lately of a worn and sorely tried American student who used to fly to a certain German word for relief when he could bear up under his aggravations no longer – the only word whose *sound* was sweet and precious to his ear and healing to his lacerated spirit. This was the word *Damit*. It was only the sound that helped him, not the meaning (It merely means, in its general sense, 'herewith'); and so, at last, when he learned that the emphasis was not on the first syllable, his only stay and support was gone, and he faded away and died.

I think that a description of any loud, stirring, tumultuous episode must be tamer in German than in English. Our descriptive words of this character have such a deep, strong, resonant sound, while their German equivalents do seem so thin and mild and energyless. Boom, burst, crash, roar, storm, bellow, blow, thunder, explosion, howl, cry, shout, yell, groan, battle, hell. These are magnificent words; they have a force and magnitude of sound befitting the things which they describe. But their German equivalents would be ever so nice to sing the children to sleep with, or else my awe-inspiring ears were made for display and not for superior usefulness in analyzing sounds. Would any man want to die in a battle which was called by so tame a term as a *Schlacht*? Or would not a consumptive feel too much bundled up, who was about to go out, in a shirt-collar and a seal-ring, into a storm which the bird-song word *Gewitter* was employed to describe? And observe the strongest of the several German equivalents for explosion – *Ausbruch*. Our word toothbrush is more powerful than that. It seems to me that the Germans could do worse than import it into their language to describe particularly tremendous explosions with. The German word for hell – *Hoelle* – sounds more like helly than anything else; therefore, how necessarily chipper, frivolous, and unimpressive it is. If a man were told in German to go there, could he really rise to the dignity of feeling insulted?

Having pointed out, in detail, the several vices of this language, I now come to the brief and pleasant task of pointing out its virtues. The capitalizing of the nouns I have already mentioned. But far before this virtue stands another – that of spelling a word according to the sound of it. After one short lesson in the alphabet, the student can tell how any German word is pronounced without having to ask; whereas in our language if a student should inquire of us, 'What does B, O, W, spell?' we should be obliged to reply, 'Nobody can tell what it spells when you set if off by itself; you can only tell by referring to the context and finding out what it signifies – whether it is a thing to shoot arrows with, or a nod of one's head, or the forward end of a boat.'

There are some German words which are singularly and powerfully effective. For instance, those which describe lowly, peaceful, and affectionate home life; those which deal with love, in any and all forms, from mere kindly feeling and honest good will toward the passing stranger, clear up to courtship; those which deal with outdoor Nature, in its softest and loveliest aspects – with meadows and forests, and birds and flowers, the fragrance and sunshine of summer, and the moonlight of peaceful winter nights; in a word, those which deal with any and all forms of rest, repose, and peace; those also which deal with the creatures and marvels of fairyland; and lastly and chiefly, in those words which express pathos, is the language surpassingly rich and affective. There are German songs which can make a stranger to the language cry. That shows that the *sound* of the words is correct – it interprets the meanings with truth and with exactness; and so the ear is informed, and through the ear, the heart.

The Germans do not seem to be afraid to repeat a word when it is the right one. They repeat it several times, if they choose. That is wise. But in English, when we have used a word a couple of times in a paragraph, we imagine we are growing tautological, and so we are weak enough to exchange it for some other word which only approximates exactness, to escape what we wrongly fancy is a greater blemish. Repetition may be bad, but surely inexactness is worse.

There are people in the world who will take a great deal of trouble to point out the faults in a religion or a language, and then go blandly about their business without suggesting any remedy. I am not that kind of person. I have shown that the German language needs reforming. Very well, I am ready to reform it. At least I am ready to make the proper suggestions. Such a course as this might be immodest in another; but I have devoted upward of nine full weeks, first and last, to a careful and critical study of this tongue, and thus have acquired a confidence in my ability to reform it which no mere superficial culture could have conferred upon me.

In the first place, I would leave out the dative case. It confuses the plurals; and, besides, nobody ever knows when he is in the dative case, except he discover it by accident – and then he does not know when or where it was that he got into it, or how long he has been in it, or how he is ever going to get out of it again. The dative case is but an ornamental folly – it is better to discard it.

In the next place, I would move the Verb further up to the front. You may load up with ever so good a verb, but I notice that you never really bring down a subject with it at the present German range – you only cripple it. So I insist that this important part of speech should be brought forward to a position where it may be easily seen with the naked eye.

Thirdly, I would import some strong words from the English tongue – to swear with, and also to use in describing all sorts of vigorous things in a vigorous way. 'Verdammt', and its variations and enlargements, are words which have plenty of meaning, but the *sounds* are so mild and ineffectual that German ladies can use them without sin. German ladies who could not be induced to commit a sin by any persuasion or compulsion, promptly rip out one of these harmless little words when they tear their dresses or don't like the soup. It sounds about as wicked as our 'My gracious'. German ladies are constantly saying, 'Ach! Gott!' 'Mein Gott!' 'Gott in Himmel!' 'Herr Gott' 'Der Herr Jesus!' etc. They think our ladies have the same custom, perhaps; for I once heard a gentle and lovely old German lady say to a sweet young

American girl: 'The two languages are so alike – how pleasant that is; we say "Ach! Gott!" you say "Goddamn".'

Fourthly, I would reorganizes the sexes, and distribute them accordingly to the will of the creator. This as a tribute of respect, if nothing else.

Fifthly, I would do away with those great long compounded words; or require the speaker to deliver them in sections, with intermissions for refreshments. To wholly do away with them would be best, for ideas are more easily received and digested when they come one at a time than when they come in bulk. Intellectual food is like any other; it is pleasanter and more beneficial to take it with a spoon than with a shovel.

Sixthly, I would require a speaker to stop when he is done, and not hang a string of those useless '*haven sind gewesen gehabt haben geworden seins*' to the end of his oration. This sort of gewgaws undignify a speech, instead of adding a grace. They are, therefore, an offense, and should be discarded.

Seventhly, I would discard the Parenthesis. Also the reparenthesis, the re-reparenthesis, and the re-re-re-re-re-reparentheses, and likewise the final wide-reaching all-enclosing king-parenthesis. I would require every individual, be he high or low, to unfold a plain straightforward tale, or else coil it and sit on it and hold his peace. Infractions of this law should be punishable with death.

And eighthly, and last, I would retain Zug and Schlag, with their pendants, and discard the rest of the vocabulary. This would simplify the language.

I have now named what I regard as the most necessary and important changes. These are perhaps all I could be expected to name for nothing; but there are other suggestions which I can and will make in case my proposed application shall result in my being formally employed by the government in the work of reforming the language.

My philological studies have satisfied me that a gifted person ought to learn English (barring spelling and pronouncing) in thirty hours, French in thirty days, and German in thirty years.

It seems manifest, then, that the latter tongue ought to be trimmed down and repaired. If it is to remain as it is, it ought to be gently and reverently set aside among the dead languages, for only the dead have time to learn it.

Switzerland

We located ourselves at the Jungfrau Hotel, one of those huge establishments which the needs of modern travel have created in every attractive spot on the continent. There was a great gathering at dinner, and, as usual, one heard all sorts of languages.

The table d'hôte was served by waitresses dressed in the quaint and comely costume of the Swiss peasants. This consists of a simple *gros de laine*, trimmed with ashes of roses, with overskirt of *scaré bleu ventre saint gris*, cut bias on the off-side, with facings of petit polonaise and narrow insertions of *pâté de foie gras* backstitched to the *mise en scène* in the form of a *jeu d'esprit*. It gives to the wearer a singularly piquant and alluring aspect.

One of these waitresses, a woman of forty, had side-whiskers reaching half-way down her jaws. They were two fingers broad, dark in color, pretty thick, and the hairs were an inch long. One sees many women on the continent with quite conspicuous mustaches, but this was the only woman I saw who had reached the dignity of whiskers.

After dinner the guests of both sexes distributed themselves about the front porches and the ornamental grounds belonging to the hotel, to enjoy the cool air; but, as the twilight deepened toward darkness, they gathered themselves together in that saddest and solemnest and most constrained of all places, the great blank drawing room which is the chief feature of all continental summer hotels. There they grouped themselves about, in couples and threes, and mumbled in bated voices, and looked timid and homeless and forlorn.

There was a small piano in this room, a clattery, wheezy, asthmatic thing, certainly the very worst miscarriage in the way of a piano that the world has seen. In turn, five or six dejected and homesick ladies approached it doubtingly, gave it a single inquiring thump, and retired with the lockjaw. But the boss of that instrument was to come, nevertheless; and from my own country – from Arkansas.

She was a brand-new bride, innocent, girlish, happy in herself and her grave and worshiping stripling of a husband; she was about eighteen, just out of school, free from affectations, unconscious of that passionless multitude around her; and the very first time she smote that old wreck one recognized that it had met its destiny. Her stripling brought an armful of aged sheet-music from their room – for this bride went 'heeled', as you might say – and bent himself lovingly over and got ready to turn the pages.

The bride fetched a swoop with her fingers from one end of the keyboard to the other, just to get her bearings, as it were, and you could see the congregation set their teeth with the agony of it. Then, without any more preliminaries, she turned on all the horrors of the 'Battle of Prague', that venerable shivaree, and waded chin-deep in the blood of the slain. She made a fair and honorable average of two false notes in every five, but her soul was in arms and she never stopped to correct. The audience stood it with pretty fair grit for a while, but when the cannonade waxed hotter and fiercer, and the discord average rose to four in five, the procession began to move. A few stragglers held their ground ten minutes longer, but when the girl began to wring the true inwardness out of the 'cries of the wounded', they struck their colors and retired in a kind of panic.

There never was a completer victory; I was the only non-combatant left on the field. I would not have deserted my countrywoman anyhow, but indeed I had no desires in that direction. None of us like mediocrity, but we all reverence perfection. This girl's music was perfection in its way; it was the worst music that had ever been achieved on our planet by a mere human being.

I moved up close, and never lost a strain. When she got through, I asked her to play it again. She did it with a pleased alacrity and a heightened enthusiasm. She made it *all* discords, this time. She got an amount of anguish into the cries of the wounded that shed a new light on human suffering. She was on the warpath all the evening. All the time, crowds of people gathered on the porches and pressed their noses against the windows to look and marvel, but the bravest never ventured in. The bride went off satisfied and happy with her young fellow, when her appetite was finally gorged, and the tourists swarmed in again.

What a change has come over Switzerland, and in fact all Europe, during this century! Seventy or eighty years ago Napoleon was the only man in Europe who could really be called a traveler; he was the only man who had devoted his attention to it and taken a powerful interest in it; he was the only man who had traveled extensively; but now everybody goes everywhere; and Switzerland, and many other regions which were unvisited and unknown remotenesses a hundred years ago, are in our days a buzzing hive of restless strangers every summer. But I digress.

In the morning, when we looked out of our windows, we saw a wonderful sight. Across the valley, and apparently quite neighborly and close at hand, the giant form of the Jungfrau rose cold and white into the clear sky, beyond a gateway in the nearer highlands. It reminded me, somehow, of one of those colossal billows which swells suddenly up beside one's ship, at sea, sometimes, with its crest and shoulders snowy white, and the rest of its noble proportions streaked downward with creamy foam.

I took out my sketchbook and made a little picture of the Jungfrau, merely to get the shape.

I do not regard this as one of my finished works, in fact I do not rank it among my Works at all; it is only a study; it is hardly more than what one might call a sketch. Other artists have done me the grace to admire it; but I am severe in my judgments of my own pictures, and this one does not move me.

It was hard to believe that that lofty wooded rampart on the left which so overtops the Jungfrau was not actually the higher of the two, but it was not, of course. It is only 2,000 or 3,000 feet high, and of course has no snow upon it in summer, whereas the

Jungfrau is not much shorter of 14,000 feet high and therefore that lowest verge of snow on her side, which seems nearly down to the valley level, is really about 7,000 feet higher up in the air than the summit of that wooded rampart. It is the distance that makes the deception. The wooded height is but four or five miles removed from us, but the Jungfrau is four or five times that distance away.

Walking down the street of shops, in the fore-noon, I was attracted by a large picture, carved, frame and all, from a single block of chocolate-colored wood. There are people who know everything. Some of these had told us that continental shopkeepers always raise their prices on English and Americans. Many people had told us it was expensive to buy things through a courier, whereas I had supposed it was just the reverse. When I saw this picture, I conjectured that it was worth more than the friend I proposed to buy it for would like to pay, but still it was worthwhile to inquire; so I told the courier to step in and ask the price, as if he wanted it for himself; I told him not to speak in English, and above all not to reveal the fact that he was a courier. Then I moved on a few yards, and waited.

The courier came presently and reported the price. I said to myself, 'It is a hundred francs too much' and so dismissed the matter from my mind. But in the afternoon I was passing that place with Harris, and the picture attracted me again. We stepped in, to see how much higher broken German would raise the price. The shopwoman named a figure just a hundred francs lower than the courier had named. This was a pleasant surprise. I said I would take it. After I had given directions as to where it was to be shipped, the shopwoman said, appealingly:

'If you please, do not let your courier know you bought it.'

This was an unexpected remark. I said:

'What makes you think I have a courier?'

'Ah, that is very simple; he told me himself.'

'He was very thoughtful. But tell me – why did you charge him more than you are charging me?'

'That is very simple, also: I do not have to pay you a percentage.'

'Oh, I begin to see. You would have had to pay the courier a percentage.'

'Undoubtedly. The courier always has his percentage. In this case it would have been a hundred francs.'

'Then the tradesman does not pay a part of it – the purchaser pays all of it?'

'There are occasions when the tradesman and the courier agree upon a price which is twice or thrice the value of the article, then the two divide, and both get a percentage.'

'I see. But it seems to me that the purchaser does all the paying, even then.'

'Oh, to be sure! It goes without saying.'

'But I have bought this picture myself; therefore why shouldn't the courier know it?'

The woman exclaimed, in distress:

'Ah, indeed it would take all my little profit! He would come and demand his hundred francs, and I should have to pay.'

'He has not done the buying. You could refuse.'

'I could not dare to refuse. He would never bring travelers here again. More than that, he would denounce me to the other couriers, they would divert custom from me, and my business would be injured.'

I went away in a thoughtful frame of mind. I began to see why a courier could afford to work for fifty-five dollars a month and his fares. A month or two later I was able to understand why a courier did not have to pay any board and lodging, and why my hotel bills were always larger when I had him with me than when I left him behind, somewhere, for a few days.

Another thing was also explained, now, apparently. In one town I had taken the courier to the bank to do the translating when I drew some money. I had sat in the reading-room till the transaction was finished. Then a clerk had brought the money to me in person, and had been exceedingly polite, even going so far as to precede me to the door and holding it open for me and bow me out as if I had been a distinguished personage. It was a new experience. Exchange had been in my favor ever since I had been in Europe, but just that one time. I got simply the face of my draft, and no extra francs, whereas I had expected to get quite a number of them. This was the first time I had ever used the courier at the bank. I had suspected something then, and as long as he remained with me afterward I managed bank matters by myself.

Still, if I felt that I could afford the tax, I would never travel without a courier, for a good courier is a convenience whose value cannot be estimated in dollars and cents. Without him, travel is a bitter harassment, a purgatory of little exasperating annoyances, a ceaseless and pitiless punishment – I mean to an irascible man who has no business capacity and is confused by details.

Without a courier, travel hasn't a ray of pleasure in it, anywhere; but with him it is a continuous and unruffled delight. He is always at hand, never has to be sent for; if your bell is not answered promptly – and it seldom is – you have only to open the door and speak, the courier will hear, and he will have the order attended to or raise an insurrection. You tell him what day you will start, and whither you are going – leave all the rest to him. You need not inquire about trains, or fares, or car changes, or hotels, or anything else. At the proper time he will put you in a cab or an omnibus, and drive you to the train or the boat; he has packed your luggage and transferred it, he has paid all the bills. Other people have preceded you half an hour to scramble for impossible places and lose their tempers, but you can take your time; the courier has secured your seats for you, and you can occupy them at your leisure.

At the station, the crowd mash one another to pulp in the effort to get the weigher's attention to their trunks; they dispute hotly with these tyrants, who are cool and indifferent; they get their baggage billets, at last, and then have another squeeze and another rage over the disheartening business of trying to get them recorded and paid for, and still another over the equally disheartening business of trying to get near enough to the ticket office to buy a ticket; and now, with their tempers gone to the dogs, they must stand penned up and packed together, laden with wraps and satchels and shawl-straps, with the weary wife and babies, in the waiting room, till the doors are thrown open – and then all hands make a grand final rush to the train, find it full, and have to stand on the platform and fret until some more cars are put on. They are in a condition to kill somebody by this time. Meantime, you have been sitting in your car, smoking, and observing all this misery in the extremest comfort.

On the journey the guard is polite and watchful – won't allow anybody to get into your compartment – tells them you are just recovering from the smallpox and do not like to be disturbed. For the courier has made everything right with the guard. At waystations the courier comes to your compartment to see if you want a glass of water, or a newspaper, or anything; at eating stations he sends luncheon out to you, while the other people scramble and worry in the dining rooms. If anything breaks about the car you are in, and a station master proposes to pack you and your agent into a compartment with strangers, the courier reveals to him confidentially that you are a French duke born deaf and dumb, and the official comes and makes affable signs that he has ordered a choice car to be added to the train for you.

At custom houses the multitude file tediously through, hot and irritated, and look on while the officers burrow into the trunks and make a mess of everything; but you hand your keys to the courier and sit still. Perhaps you arrive at your destination in a rainstorm at ten at night – you generally do. The multitude spend half an hour verifying their baggage and getting it transferred to the omnibuses; but the courier puts you into a vehicle without a moment's loss of time, and when you reach your hotel you find your rooms have been secured two or three days in advance, everything is ready, you can go at once to bed. Some of those other people will have to drift around to two or three hotels, in the rain, before they find accommodations.

I have not set down half of the virtues that are vested in a good courier, but I think I have set down a sufficiency of them to show that an irritable man who can afford one and does not employ him is not a wise economist. My courier was the worst one in Europe, yet he was a good deal better than none at all. It could not pay him to be a better one than he was, because I could not afford to buy things through him. He was a good enough courier for the small amount he got out of his service. Yes, to travel with a courier is bliss, to travel without one is the reverse.

I have had dealings with some very bad couriers; but I have also had dealings with one who might fairly be called perfection. He was a young Polander, named Joseph N. Verey. He spoke eight languages, and seemed to be equally at home in all of them; he was shrewd, prompt, posted, and punctual; he was fertile in resources, and singularly gifted in the matter of overcoming difficulties; he not only knew how to do everything in his line, but he knew the best ways and the quickest; he was handy with children and invalids; all his employer needed to do was to take life easy and leave everything to the courier. His address is, care of Messrs. Gay & Son, Strand, London; he was formerly a conductor of Gay's tourist parties. Excellent couriers are somewhat rare; if the reader is about to travel, he will find it to his advantage to make a note of this one.

Notes

Notes

i   Literally 'Host's Table', a meal served in a guesthouse. (Fr.)

ii   'Here we speak French.' (Fr.)

iii   Working class women, independent figures, they often doubled as artists' models – and were thought to be sexually promiscuous. (Fr.)

iv   Begone!

v   Porter (It.)

vi   Farmer, husbandman (It.)

vii   Machine gun (Fr.)

viii   Colazione is Italian for a collection, a meeting, a seance, a sitting. [This is Mark Twain's own note.]

Biographical Note

Mark Twain was born Samuel Langhorne Clemens in 1835 in Florida. Soon after his birth his family moved to Hannibal, Missouri, where he spent his childhood. Following his father's death in 1847, Twain worked as a printer for a newspaper owned by his brother, before finding employment in New York and Philadelphia, again as a printer. From 1857 to 1861, he worked as a river pilot on the Mississippi, before moving firstly to Virginia City, and then to California to take up a position as a newspaper correspondent. A successful short story in 1865 quickly inspired a collection entitled 'The Celebrated Jumping Frog of Calaveras County, and Other Sketches' (1867), and further volumes swiftly followed. With striking effect, Twain prioritised the method of telling a story over its outcome, and, though a prolific writer of satires, travelogues, essays, and letters, he is best remembered for his picaresque depictions of Missouri life: namely his 1876 novel, *The Adventures of Tom Sawyer*, and its sequel, *The Adventures of Huckleberry Finn* (1884).

In 1870 Twain married Olivia Langdon. Her death in 1904, together with the loss of their daughter, Susy, and the onset of financial difficulties in the 1890s, had an impact on Twain's later work; potboilers were written for money, and other works became darker in tone. Twain spent much of the 1890s in Europe, residing by turns in England, Switzerland, Austria and France, before returning to New York in 1900 and then settling in Connecticut. He died on 21 April 1910.

SELECTED TITLES FROM HESPERUS PRESS

Author	Title	Foreword writer
Pietro Aretino	*The School of Whoredom*	Paul Bailey
Pietro Aretino	*The Secret Life of Nuns*	
Jane Austen	*Lesley Castle*	Zoë Heller
Jane Austen	*Love and Friendship*	Fay Weldon
Honoré de Balzac	*Colonel Chabert*	A.N.Wilson
Charles Baudelaire	*On Wine and Hashish*	Margaret Drabble
Giovanni Boccaccio	*Life of Dante*	A.N.Wilson
Charlotte Brontë	*The Spell*	
Emily Brontë	*Poems of Solitude*	Helen Dunmore
Mikhail Bulgakov	*Fatal Eggs*	Doris Lessing
Mikhail Bulgakov	*The Heart of a Dog*	A.S. Byatt
Giacomo Casanova	*The Duel*	Tim Parks
Miguel de Cervantes	*The Dialogue of the Dogs*	Ben Okri
Geoffrey Chaucer	*The Parliament of Birds*	
Anton Chekhov	*The Story of a Nobody*	Louis de Bernières
Anton Chekhov	*Three Years*	William Fiennes
Wilkie Collins	*The Frozen Deep*	
Joseph Conrad	*Heart of Darkness*	A.N.Wilson
Joseph Conrad	*The Return*	Colm Tóibín
Gabriele D'Annunzio	*The Book of the Virgins*	Tim Parks
Dante Alighieri	*The Divine Comedy: Inferno*	
Dante Alighieri	*New Life*	Louis de Bernières
Daniel Defoe	*The King of Pirates*	Peter Ackroyd
Marquis de Sade	*Incest*	Janet Street-Porter
Charles Dickens	*The Haunted House*	PeterA ckroyd
Charles Dickens	*A House to Let*	
Fyodor Dostoevsky	*The Double*	Jeremy Dyson
Fyodor Dostoevsky	*Poor People*	Charlotte Hobson
Alexandre Dumas	*One Thousand and One Ghosts*	
George Eliot	*Amos Barton*	Matthew Sweet
Henry Fielding	*Jonathan Wild the Great*	Pete Ackroyd

F. Scott Fitzgerald	*The Popular Girl*	Helen Dunmore
Gustave Flaubert	*Memoirs of a Madman*	Germaine Greer
Ugo Foscolo	*Last Letters of Jacopo Ortis*	Valerio Massimo Manfredi
Elizabeth Gaskell	*Lois the Witch*	Jenny Uglow
Théophile Gautier	*The Jinx*	Gilbert Adair
André Gide	*Theseus*	
Johann Wolfgang von Goethe	*The Man of Fifty*	A.S. Byatt
NikolaiGogol	*The Squabble*	Patrick McCabe
E.T.A. Hoffmann	Mademoiselle de Scudéri	Gilbert Adair
Victor Hugo	*The Last Day of a Condemned Man*	Libby Purves
Joris-Karl Huysmans	*With the Flow*	Simon Callow
Henry James	*In the Cage*	Libby Purves
Franz Kafka	*Metamorphosis*	Martin Jarvis
Franz Kafka	*The Trial*	Zadie Smith
John Keats	*Fugitive Poems*	Andrew Motion
Heinrich von Kleist	*TheMarquise of O–*	Andrew Miller
Mikhail Lermontov	*A Hero of OurTime*	Doris Lessing
Nikolai Leskov	*Lady Macbeth of Mtsensk*	Gilbert Adair
Carlo Levi	*Words are Stones*	Anita Desai
Xavier deMaistre	*A Journey Around my Room*	Alain de Botton
André Malraux	*The Way of the Kings*	Rachel Seiffert
Katherine Mansfield	*Prelude*	William Boyd
Edgar Lee Masters	*Spoon River Anthology*	Shena Mackay
Guy de Maupassant	*Butterball*	Germaine Greer
Prosper Mérimée	*Carmen*	Philip Pullman
Sir Thomas More	*The History of King Richard III*	Sister Wendy Beckett
Sándor Petöfi	*John the Valiant*	George Szirtes
Francis Petrarch	*My Secret Book*	Germaine Greer
Luigi Pirandello	*Loveless Love*	
Edgar Allan Poe	*Eureka*	Sir Patrick Moore
Alexander Pope	*The Rape of the Lock and A Key to the Lock*	Peter Ackroyd

Antoine-François Prévost	*Manon Lescaut*	Germaine Greer
Marcel Proust	*Pleasures and Days*	A.N.Wilson
Alexander Pushkin	*Dubrovsky*	Patrick Neate
Alexander Pushkin	*Ruslan and Lyudmila*	Colm Tóibín
François Rabelais	*Pantagruel*	Paul Bailey
François Rabelais	*Gargantua*	Paul Bailey
Christina Rossetti	*Commonplace*	Andrew Motion
George Sand	*The Devil's Pool*	Victoria Glendinning
Jean-Paul Sartre	*The Wall*	Justin Cartwright
Friedrich von Schiller	*The Ghost-seer*	Martin Jarvis
Mary Shelley	*Transformation*	
Percy Bysshe Shelley	*Zastrozzi*	Germaine Greer
Stendhal	*Memoirs of an Egotist*	Doris Lessing
Robert Louis Stevenson	*Dr Jekyll and Mr Hyde*	Helen Dunmore
Theodor Storm	*The Lake of the Bees*	Alan Sillitoe
Leo Tolstoy	The Death of Ivan Ilych	
Leo Tolstoy	Hadji Murat	Colm Tóibín
IvanTurgenev	*Faust*	Simon Callow
Mark Twain	*The Diary of Adam and Eve*	John Updike
Mark Twain	*Tom Sawyer, Detective*	
Oscar Wilde	*The Portrait of Mr W.H.*	Peter Ackroyd
Virginia Woolf	*Carlyle's House and Other Sketches*	Doris Lessing
Virginia Woolf	*Monday or Tuesday*	Scarlett Thomas
Emile Zola	*For a Night of Love*	A.N.Wilson